Di

Martin Smy

Loyalties

Alan Beith   Michael Alison

Shared

Alistair Burt   Betty Mawhinney

Beliefs

Donald Anderson   Andrew Welsh

John G Muir

C·F·P

Christian·Focus·Publications

to my wife
Gwen

© 1994 John G. Muir
ISBN 1-85792-100-3

Published by
Christian Focus Publications Ltd
Geanies House, Fearn, Ross-shire,
IV20 1TW, Scotland, Great Britain.

Printed and bound in Great Britain by
Cox & Wyman Ltd, Reading, Berkshire

Cover design by Donna Macleod

The hymn entitled *God of our Divided World* is from the Church
Hymnary (Third Edition) Hymn no 506 Copyright Alan. N.
Phillips By kind permission of the author.

The hymn entitled *O Lord, all the world belongs to you*, Words
and Music: Patrick Appleforth 1965 © Josef Weinberger Ltd
Originally printed in '27 20th Century Hymns' Reproduced by
permission of the copyright owners

Contents

God of our Divided World

O God of our divided world,
Light up the way where our ways part.
Restore the kinship of our birth,
Revive in us a single heart -

A heart that sees in Christ its goal
And cares with Christ for every man,
That seeks beyond all outward forms
The brotherhood of God's own plan.

Where we have failed to understand
Our brother's heart, O Lord, forgive.
Grant us the confidence to share
The lights whereby our brothers live.

Then shall we know a richer world
Where all divisions are disowned,
Where heart joins heart and hand joins hand,
Where man is loved and Christ enthroned.

Alan Norman Phillips (1910 -)

Foreword
by
The Lord Chancellor
Lord Mackay of Clashfern

It is a privilege to provide a foreword for this contribution by Members of Parliament, from different political parties and from a variety of backgrounds, describing the way in which their Christian beliefs affect their work.

Pressures on Members in Westminster make it very difficult for them to maintain an ordinary family life however much they might wish to do so. Therefore, an important part of this book is the contribution by Betty Mawhinney on the place of the Parliamentary Wives Christian Fellowship. This fellowship supports parliamentary wives under the special burdens caused by the public service on which their spouses are engaged. The concluding chapter of the book with the author's view of the present situation in our country is one which must challenge everyone interested in the well being of the United Kingdom of Great Britain and Northern Ireland and its place in the world.

It has been fascinating for me to read the accounts given to John Muir by so many of my distinguished colleagues in Westminster. I think that readers will find stimulating the insights given on how individual Members of Parliament approach their responsibilities and also into the power of Christian principles in shaping them.

These principles form a bond of union between those who have contributed, which is deep and strong, and which give them a concern for one another even if they do not support the same political party. It is surely very striking that each sees the work he is doing in his own party as being in accord with his Christian principles. This emphasises a message repeatedly stressed by those interviewed, that they do not regard Christianity as an election manifesto for any particular political party. No political party can claim that it alone has the sanction of Christianity. Indeed the contributors are careful to point out that it is apt to debase a Christian's stand if he seeks to link it in too specific a manner to the political philosophy of his party. On the other hand it is pointed out that those who are Christians ought not to hide their light or conceal that fact in describing themselves in their claims for the attention of the electorate.

The author emphasises that the issues facing Members of Parliament, and any who have responsibility in Government in our country in these times, are extremely complex. However deep their faith or precise their theology, they cannot expect that faith to provide a unique or glib answer to the problems our country faces today. This I think demonstrates that the idea of politicians committed to Christianity linking together to provide political leadership for the nation under the banner of Christianity is not attainable nor is it in accordance with the spirit of Christianity itself.

What I think this book shows is that Christianity is a living faith which can motivate individuals to seek the highest standards of morality and integrity in their lives, depending not upon their own strength or wisdom but looking to the Lord Jesus Christ to lead them in the right way. Individuals so motivated will be an influence for good in their families and in whatever sphere of human endeavour they may participate. To have individuals so motivated called to public service, will therefore lead to the application of these standards in public life; although, as this book demonstrates, the application of these standards will not necessarily lead to unanimity of view as to the right way forward in relation to all the problems facing our country. They will lead to mutual respect for the different points of view which these principles may embrace. This can only tend to raise to a constructive level the debate about these issues.

These accounts show in a very special way that the Members of Parliament interviewed have a strong commitment to Christianity. They are conscious of their need for divine guidance and wisdom, their need to pray over the issues that confront them and a desire to do what is right in the light of the teachings of our Lord and of the scriptures as a whole.

The book also shows that a difficult problem confronts a legislator who is fully persuaded in his own mind of the rightness of Christian principles, for example in relation to the Lord's Day. It is obvious that individuals cannot be made Christians by force of law and that the organs of the state for the enforcement of law are altogether unequal to the task of making our people Christian. People can only become Christian by hearty acceptance of the authority of our Lord Jesus Christ for themselves. While persuasion, and particularly the example of Christian living in those prominent in public life, may be powerful influences in that direction, there is a limit to what can be achieved by legislation. At the same time it has to be acknowledged that legislation may send a message to our people of what Parliament regards as acceptable conduct.

Further, it becomes clear that Christians called to serve as Members of Parliament have very considerable opportunity to commend our Lord Jesus and his message to the people they serve: by their access to the media; by their influence on the national scene and in their own constituencies; but particularly by the way they live. This message is that the real leader, the one from whom ultimately guidance is to be sought, is our Lord himself by the teaching of his Word by the illumination of the Holy Spirit.

The contributions which have been gathered should encourage everyone who reads them to embrace the message of the gospel. They will find in it a motivating principle to live useful lives in service to others in whatever sphere of endeavour may be theirs. God will be honoured as they seek to carry the principles of the gospel into every action of daily life and serve their fellow beings with love and devotion. In so living, they will respect the views of others while at the same time carrying forward their own convictions with fervency and humility in a way which will inspire confidence in all those with whom they come in contact.

Another message of this publication is that those who serve us as Members of Parliament need our prayers. It is a duty on all whom they serve in this way to pray for them, understanding that they are fallible human beings. If they give occasion for criticism, that criticism should be put forward in a constructive and helpful spirit.

We live in a time when destructive criticism, looking for scapegoats and heads to roll is all too common. I hope this book will lead to a greater understanding of the onerous responsibilities which our Members of Parliament carry and of the commitment to public service which inspires them to seek to discharge these responsibilities well. I trust also that it will encourage a spirit of cooperation and help to them rather than one of destructive negativism.

1
PAUL BOATENG
Labour MP for Brent South

In The Community, For The Community

It was 1966 and the political situation in Ghana under Dr Kwame Nkrumah was deteriorating rapidly. Kwaku Boateng, a respected government minister and lawyer in Accra was arrested by the police for his political beliefs, after a successful coup d'état. Now facing an uncertain future, Mrs Boateng knew that she had little alternative but to leave the country that she had come to love with her children and return to her native Britain, joining the growing number of political refugees who had already fled abroad to escape persecution.

Paul Boateng was fifteen when he arrived in England with his mother and sister. All that remained of their belongings was crammed into two large suitcases. It was an experience which the teenager would never forget; one, indeed, which would shape his political thinking in the years that lay ahead of him.

Born in Hackney to a Scottish mother and a Ghanaian father, Paul was only two and a half years old when the family went to Africa to set up home in what was, in Colonial days, then called the Gold Coast. Paul grew up in a household with a background in politics. His father started a legal practice in Accra and became the solicitor for the main independence movement, the Convention People's Party. His mother, whose family originally came from Midlothian in Scotland, also was active in the Labour Party in London before she moved abroad.

Paul's parents are committed Christians and one of the first things that he remembers from those early days in Africa is his baptism in the little village church.

'My grandfather had been led to Christ by Basle missionaries who were followed in the village by Scottish Presbyterians who continue to have strong links with the Ghanaian church. Until the late sixties, the Christian bookshop in Accra was run by a Scot, George Inwood, with whose family we still maintain personal contact.

'In Ghana, religion is very much a communal affair. My father wanted to wait until he returned to his home village to have me baptised. Not many children can remember their christening but I was almost five years old. I can still see the tiny building crammed with worshippers inside and surrounded by people outside who, unable to get a seat, strained to participate in the service through the open windows.

'I recall the minister saying, "Lord, we deliver this child up into your arms now for safekeeping" and, in my innocence, I envisaged God coming down there and then to take me up and away from my parents. Not unnaturally, I started to scream and shout while I tried to make a run for it! I was extremely relieved to find out that, despite the pleas of the minister to the Almighty, I remained in the church, with my feet firmly on the ground.

'The church played a central part in my life then, as it does now. As I grew up in Accra, Sunday School was something I looked forward to every week as a place to meet friends as well as learn about the Bible. Families would go down to the beach together after services for recreation and fellowship. As our faith was a source of joy and inspiration, so religion was not a bore nor church-going a chore for me. The Ridge Church which we attended was interdenominational and members of the Protestant community from a variety of church backgrounds gathered together for regular worship. It was an outgoing, lively congregation and proved to be a great strength to us when the political scene changed for the worse.'

Paul's father, having begun as a lawyer to the Convention People's Party, eventually became a member of parliament and later a cabinet minister in the government of the newly independent Ghana. He was therefore in the thick of the action when Nkrumah became a virtual dictator in a one party state.

'It was during this time, following the coup d'état, that my father was thrown into prison without trial, our house seized and the rest of the family forced to flee the country. During this difficult period in our lives, our faith sustained us and enabled my father to retain his sanity in the prison cell where he was held, not knowing whether he was going to be kept for years in custody or killed as some others were. He knew they would never try him as they had no evidence against him.

'We also valued the strength which God gave us when we had to make the transition into life in Britain, unsure whether my father would ever return among us again. The contrast with our life in Ghana was quite stark. We came from a large house with lovely gardens and servants to care for us, to a traditional two-up, two-down, semi-detached council house in Hemel Hempstead, a new town in Hertfordshire.

'My father was eventually released after nearly four years in prison. I did not see it particularly then as an answer to prayer as many who opposed the regime were not so fortunate, but my father certainly did and his was indeed an example of how faith can help one to endure privation.'

Aware of the worsening political situation, Peggy Boateng had prepared her family as best she could for such an eventuality. Nevertheless, it was a pretty traumatic experience for them. There was, of course, the continuing worry about their father and what might happen to him. The church played an important part in helping Paul to come to terms with their new way of life, not only as a place of solace and refuge but also in underpinning his political thinking at that time.

'It was 1968, the time of the civil rights movement, which coincided with the growing fight against apartheid and racism, in South Africa and in the United Kingdom. These were the days when Enoch Powell had a regular platform in the media following his now famous "Rivers of Blood" speech. As a refugee family this was a very difficult time for us and I never underestimate the help and support we found in our faith and in the Anglican congregation we joined. As one with a particular interest in music, I recall being greatly inspired by the hymns which we learned and sang there. I became part of a madrigal group which sang in churches all over Hertfordshire. As in Africa, I found friendship and fellowship under the banner of the church I attended.

'During this time also, Martin Luther-King was a great hero of mine as was Nelson Mandela, both of whom came from backgrounds of active Christian witness and relied on their faith to sustain them in difficult periods in history. I see it as central that the church should be an integral part of the community, whether it be lively and evangelical or high Anglican in its form of worship. It must engage with society, as religion is not only about personal salvation, but must also be a spur to action out in the world, doing Christ's business, reflecting the words of James, "Faith without works is dead".'

It was this aspect of the Methodist tradition which drew him later in the seventies to that particular denomination. A member of Harlesden Methodist church he preaches approximately one Sunday a month to congregations up and down the country. I put it to him that Methodism was perhaps seen to be more associated with Liberalism than with Socialism and he took up the debate.

'I think radical nonconformist politics is associated with one strain of Methodism; Liberalism in some areas of the country and Socialism in others. Certainly, religious nonconformity of the Wesleyan variety has often been associated with the Liberal/Labour tradition although it shouldn't be forgotten that Methodism has another strand which is very much geared towards commerce and Conservatism. It was the sense of the church working in and for the community which caught my attention and attracted me to join.'

In the early seventies, when he had qualified as a

solicitor after studying law at Bristol University, he became a lawyer at Paddington Law and Advice Centre. He chose this path because he wanted specifically to make a contribution to society, work in the community with and for people and address their needs in terms of housing, family breakdown and domestic violence.

'I began my training as a lawyer working with a woman called Tess Gill, an early feminist lawyer who worked with Erin Pizzie of the Women's Refuge Movement. Looking back I realise that I spent much of my training period running around London, being chased by husbands and wife batterers, and serving matrimonial injunctions.'

Such work did not discourage him from 'tying the knot' with his fiancée, Janet, originally from Barbados, whom he met at this time. They were later married and now have five children, three girls and two boys, ranging from a thirteen year old to the youngest who is only six.

His work as a lawyer took him into politics, albeit in a roundabout way, as he specialised in housing law when he was with the Centre and in civil liberty laws in particular. He was actively involved in opposition to the 'suss' law which had been the object of much campaigning on civil liberty grounds almost since its imposition in 1834 in the aftermath of the Napoleonic Wars. The law, widely viewed as being particularly discriminatory against vagrants and used mainly against blacks and working class people, was eventually removed from the statute books in 1981, due in no small part to the stance taken by Paul Boateng and others who worked with him.

'That placed me very much in the centre of things,'

Paul explained, 'working on housing and civil liberty issues. It brought me into contact with local authorities and Members of Parliament, particularly when I was elected to the Chair of the Westminster Community Relations Council in 1979. I had been a member of the Labour Party since I was fifteen and had been active at ward level, as a school governor and as a lawyer, latterly in partnership with Gareth Pearce, better known for her defence of the Birmingham and Guildford bombing suspects, who were jailed but later released after a judicial review of their cases.

'There came a time in 1980 when I got tired of lobbying and protesting at a distance so I decided that, with my by now substantial experience and a growing national reputation, I should consider standing for election in order to effect change more directly.'

Paul was selected to stand for Walthamstow in the General London Council and was elected in 1981, later becoming Chairman of the Police Committee and Vice Chairman of the Committee for Ethnic Minorities for five years. From being a reasonably well known young lawyer he made a name for himself in national political circles and it was proposed that he should stand for parliament in Islington in 1982. But he narrowly failed to be selected. When he was able to stand, for a marginal seat at the 1983 election, he was unsuccessful. By that time he was married with two children and living in Brixton, 'the eye of the storm' as far as civil rights disturbances were concerned then. His wife, Janet, who was Chair of Social Services in Lambeth was also a party activist.

In 1984 he was selected for the safe Labour seat of Brent South and has been able since then to increase the party vote at each election. In and out of parliament, he has been involved with various bodies. In addition to those already mentioned, he has been a member of the Labour Party National Executive Council, Sub Committee on Human Rights and Race Relations; member of the Police Training Council; and was Opposition Front Bench Spokesman on Treasury and Economic Affairs for three years. He is at present Shadow Spokesman on the Lord Chancellor's Office.

We discussed how he has seen the interaction of his political and spiritual priorities in life, and what dilemmas he has encountered himself or observed in others.

'Unlike some of my colleagues, I have not found areas where there has been a conflict of conscience. I am a committed Christian first and foremost. I try to base my life on Christian teaching and tradition and do my best, in terms of the development of my thoughts, to learn what the Bible teaches, to find inspiration and seek strength there. That has been enormously helpful in terms of addressing some of the dilemmas that exist in politics.

'How to integrate the material and the spiritual in the way that I think one must do is most challenging for me. Where so many "isms" and "ologys", whether of the left or of the right, fall down is that they fail to integrate the material and the spiritual. Consider for the moment the ideologies of the right: they are geared towards the satisfaction of the acquisitive impulse as if market forces can solve life's problems. In contrast, we can look at the perspective of the left: they maintain that the satisfaction of people's material needs, through more equal distribution of goods, for example, will of itself engender happiness.

'In my experience, both of these ideologies will fail, unless they are linked also to the recognition of people's spiritual thirst and hunger; and to the need to build a sense of community with a value system around it. I believe that was the major input of Christianity to the roots of my own party and, when we stray from this foundation, we are in danger of losing both our vision and our mission. The founders of the Labour Party were strongly influenced by the Christian values of community and of the importance of transforming society along lines which recognise the worth of self improvement while remaining aware of the need to share what one has with others. I firmly believe that these early leaders did seek to integrate the material and the spiritual.

'I have found that Christianity is a way of addressing some of the dilemmas and conflicts within politics. When there are difficult decisions to be made, we need points of reference and the church and the Bible can provide these.

'One of the greatest challenges for me as a member of the Labour Party has been coming to terms with repeated defeat at general elections; to reconcile myself to political impotence in opposition and be unable to radically influence events in the country. It would be easy to become defeatist, despondent and cynical. Christian teaching has helped to counteract these tendencies. From my study of the Gospels I have learned that I must use the talents I have, come what may, maximise my potential and seek to do good with what I have been given.

'I also realise that, if I am seeking to develop policy, in relation to the environment, for example, it helps if I have a view of the world in which mankind is seen as a guardian, recognised as having creation in trust. It also helps me develop a sharper, more positive, approach to the issue. In addition, I find that it is intellectually much more challenging and satisfying for me.

'I believe that Christ can bring things in our lives into sharper focus enabling us to see more clearly and with greater definition. Although we may not always have a clear view of the particular path to choose, there is certainly a better sense of direction overall and a greater ability to recognise the correct way when it confronts us.

'Having said that, I do not believe that the Bible contains some form of glorified and deified party political agenda but it does, nevertheless, provide a basis for a view of the world. More importantly, it reveals the challenging agenda which Christ has for us. His agenda is difficult as it requires us to engage with those who are our enemies in a way which is generally anathema to politicians. If we were willing to open ourselves to that sort of dialogue a lot of interesting things might happen in our country.

'There is Christian fellowship in the House of Commons, an area of common ground on which we can at least meet. But it would be wrong to believe that, because we meet on common ground, we necessarily always find common cause. We had an example of that recently in the House.

'Madame Speaker kindly played host to the president of the Methodist Conference and around that table were

Christians, not only of the Methodist tradition, but also of other backgrounds. There was notably deep political disagreement. A particularly challenging critique of government policy which the Methodists have produced has been deeply hurtful, if not offensive, to Conservatives within the denomination.

'The danger always for the Christian MP whose party is in power is that his or her witness may be muted for seemingly pragmatic or party political reasons. Those in power must also exercise it as custodians of a wider interest than party lines may permit. At the end of the day we must ask ourselves what is the role of the church if it doesn't, among other things, challenge society and the decision makers in the country? History has recorded the not infrequent friction between church and state and we delude ourselves if we believe that we have reached such democratic maturity that we can dispense with such dialogue. I trust that when our party is in office we will be similarly challenged by the principles and values which Christ and the church put forward.

'There are politicians who say that the church should keep out of politics but, as I see it, Christianity has something to say on every aspect of our lives and politics cannot be excluded. The church cannot but engage itself with principalities and powers in high places who must be challenged and confronted with the consequences of their actions. Where necessary the issues must be taken on board, without compromise, as I believe it is part of the prophetic vision of the church to do so.'

In his chapter in *Reclaiming the Ground, Christianity and Socialism* [1], which he wrote with the Rt. Hon. John

Smith and others, he includes thoughts along these lines:

> Our faith is deeply subversive, it puts the human spirit
> before institutions and subordinates the powers and the
> principalities to the overriding principles of love.

'That is not to say that I believe that the church has a
role in terms of endorsing one political party or another
from the pulpit or any other platform. Neither do I believe
that it behoves any political party to seek to cloak itself in
a way which sometimes occurs in the United States, as if
they are the only ones who are doing God's business on
earth. I do not believe that any political party can lay
claim to Jesus Christ as a member, nor should candidates
claim endorsement from God for their own purposes or
political ends.

'In my personal and political life the church has
provided me with a basis, a focus for my contribution to
society. It has proved to be for me a source of strength and
solace. In politics, as it was for me in law, I find that it is
a tough business where I might feel depressed and alienated were I not able to find a place of joy and inspiration.
A central support also has come in the form of friendship
and fellowship.

'The Christian life has been a way of keeping fresh
intellectually through Bible study and reading how others have come to Christ. It is always interesting to learn
how their faith and their lives reflect Him and these
accounts can be a great source of help and intellectual
challenge to me.

'I have found that an interest in Christian things is

certainly needed to keep the law alive. The study of law can be a narrowing rather than a broadening experience in life. It is very easy to believe that all that matters in politics is what happens in the Palace of Westminster, the seat of decision making. But Westminster is not the centre of all life and action. Rather, life there can be seen through a very distorted mirror, whereas through the church and Christian fellowship worldwide, we encounter a wider dimension and can gain a valuable insight into a very different and much more substantial world. More importantly, we are given a glimpse into everlasting life and eternal things which are far more important than the earthly concerns of the moment.'

Central though the church and politics are to his life, he sees recreation and family life as God given gifts to exploit also. To this end he takes time to relax whenever possible with his wife and family and enjoys walking, swimming and attending opera. The latter interest has resulted in his becoming an important member of the Board of English National Opera.

During our conversation I became aware that Paul Boateng's life has been shaped by many bitter and cruel encounters. Success as a lawyer, a respected barrister and latterly as a nationally recognised face in politics have not caused him to forget his roots or neglect his calling to champion the rights of the underdog in society. His campaign on behalf of ethnic minority groups has disturbed many who would rather cross over the road than address the issues he highlights. Many have opposed his views but it is true to say that those who may have done so, have maintained their respect for the stance that he has taken. That he is in great demand as a speaker and in debates on radio and television is witness to that.

Above all, it is encouraging to note his witness to the Christian faith in political and church circles. This service and outreach spring from his belief that the church must be in the community and that it should be its servant first and foremost. His busy political life has not deflected him from this goal.

His words, in *Reclaiming the Ground*, in many ways sum up the interesting time we had together:

> Followers of Christ cannot partition religious life and worship from involvement in the concerns of political and economic justice. Life isn't to be separated into little boxes in this way, one labelled religious and the other secular. [2]

1. *Reclaiming the Ground, Christianity and Socialism* by the Rt. Hon. John Smith and Others (1993. Spire, Hodder and Stoughton Publishers)
2. ibid.

2
THE RT. HON. MICHAEL ALISON
Conservative MP for Selby

A View From the Bridge

BILL BATT. The name on the notice board caught his eye and not only because of the rather humorous alliteration. Was the gentleman in question the major that he knew in the regiment he joined when he was called to do national service? If so, this was no army recruitment poster to encourage Oxford dons to make a career in the armed forces. It was a religious meeting which was being brought to the attention of the students of the famous university. Michael Alison decided to go along to hear what Bill Batt had to say, more out of curiosity than in recognition of any church commitment he might wish to confess to a former officer.

What was meant to be a casual chat with the major at the end of the talk, turned out to be an encounter which was to change Michael's life. The astute officer soon moved the discussion from army reminiscences to religion and the conversation began to heat up. Christianity was something Michael thought little about these days, unlike when he was a pupil at Eton.

Although his parents had Scottish roots, he was born at Margate in Kent, when they moved South of the Border in the early twenties. They attended the local Anglican church and their son was baptised into that faith. There were basic Christian influences on him in childhood and when he began his education at Eton College, religious education played a central role in his school life, reflected in compulsory, twice daily attendance at chapel. On the surface it seemed that all this had little spiritual impact on him, even after attending confirmation classes in his teens.

When he left school, and during his time as an officer in the army at the end of the war, Christianity was for Sundays and holy days, no more than the occasional ritual in recognition of his upbringing; certainly not something to get too personal about or to discuss when relaxing with friends of an evening. But these early influences were less easy to dismiss than he first thought they might be.

'In retrospect, I now see that there was a residue of influence on me by the familiar liturgy of the Church of England; by the ring of the Authorised Version of the Bible which was read to us twice a day. As new translations emerge on a regular basis, I have to say that the marvellous, quaint English of the AV sticks in my subconscious like a burr much more than a modern version does. Unknown to me I carried away in the recesses of my mind a muddle of Christian phrases, ideas and words, which became a source upon which I was able to draw many years later.'

His spell in the army over, he gained entrance to Wadham College, Oxford, where he read Politics, Philosophy and Economics, and began to focus his mind on the direction his life should take.

'Many things came to mind, particularly as my graduation drew near, but one thing was certain, I would not become a Church of England parson! All that changed when Major Bill Batt, a regular visitor to Oxford, came back into my life from my army days. When the conversation turned to Christianity I told him that it was not uppermost in my mind and I certainly let him know that, whatever career I chose, I ruled out the possibility of getting involved in the church.

'I will never forget his response to my adamancy. He was silent for a minute then, raising his eyebrows, asked, "When you were in the army as a young officer and the adjutant told you to get a haircut, did you not obey?" Of course, I replied that I certainly would, knowing that the alternative would have been to have a tin pot put on my head and my hair cut hastily round the rim!

' "Don't you think, then," the major continued, "that it is odd that you should be prepared to obey an officer, only a few years older than you, simply because he has authority and could make things uncomfortable for you? Yet you would be prepared to disobey God because He doesn't immediately make life difficult for you?"

'As far as I was concerned, God did not enter into the equation at all at this point in my life so what was this man talking about? Later I thought more about what the forthright major had to say. If I believed in God, which I suppose I did at the time, perhaps I should be thinking about some greater plan for my life.

'Shortly after this I was invited to attend a freshman's church service where the preacher was Dr John Stott. His text on that occasion was from Acts 17, Paul's speech to the assembled intellectuals in Athens; a gathering very much akin to the undergraduates he was addressing that day in Oxford: *The ignorance of this past time God winked at but he now commandeth all men everywhere to repent.*

'I recalled the rebuke of Major Batt and realised that Paul's message was not only to the Athenians of old but was also the word of God to me there and then. It was a command which I had to obey. I had an overwhelming conviction that God was speaking directly to me and realised that I had to face the realities of faith, believe in Christ and submit myself entirely to the will of God.'

From that moment Michael assumed that the last thing he wanted to do in his life - become a clergyman - was, in fact, the path God would expect him to follow. It was not easy to accept, but he gritted his teeth, nevertheless, and set his mind on studying with the Church of England as soon as he left Oxford. A few years later, he entered Ridley Hall, Cambridge, an Anglican theological college, to study for the ministry.

'Going far beyond what Major Batt and John Stott had implied in their timely words, I had the idea that the thing I least wanted to do was what God would automatically command I should do. In reality, I was totally misinterpreting not only the will of God but also His very nature. God does not deal with people in this way and I soon found myself caught up in a dreadful dilemma. There was I in the midst of a college of potential ordinands, all of whom were totally committed and longing for the day when they could commence their ministry. While they were enjoying the prospect, I felt like a Jonah in the middle of them, dreading my own Nineveh and the future ahead of me.

'In my heart of hearts, I knew that I was more interested in politics than preaching; in debating party issues than being a pastor to a congregation. But this seemed to be a somewhat less spiritual direction to take in the light of my decision to follow Christ on hearing the sermon by John Stott. After much heart-searching and sharing my concerns with the academic staff and fellow students, I was eventually persuaded that this was very unlikely to be God's call I was hearing.'

When reading politics at Oxford Michael was greatly influenced by the writings of the historian, A J P Taylor. His particular style highlighted the fact that most of the momentous events in Europe did not take place as the result of great impersonal forces like climate, geography or economics which might dictate the direction as an icepack would force a ship to navigate along a certain path. Rather, Taylor maintained, it was some very basic personal factor in leading statesmen, like jealousy, envy or ambition which drove them to decide one way or another.

As Michael mulled over this, it occurred to him what a great opportunity it would be for Christians to get into the sphere of the decision makers. At least they may be able to isolate the grosser forms of self concern and self interest and genuinely try to take decisions in a way which may be disadvantageous to them but advantageous to the common good. That was fine motivation to head off into politics as far as he was concerned.

Expanding his views on the subject, he then graphically recalled his appetite for politics at that time.

'If we think of life as being a journey on a great cruise

liner, crossing a vast ocean, there are various places we can be on that ship, according to our aptitude. Avid readers may spend their time in the liner's library; if engineering is of interest, the engine room is worth a visit; the more athletic will be in the gym or in the swimming pool; others may decide to relax, watch a film or have a meal in the dining room.

'On a few occasions as a child I was able to stand beside the captain of a large ship and I was absolutely overawed by the experience. Since then I have always thought that by far the most interesting place to be on a great liner is on the bridge. It is not easy to get there, as this is the part of the ship most usually barred to passengers. At the same time, the NO ADMITTANCE sign is an added incentive to try to get up there! What you experience on the bridge is really the most fascinating perspective you can have on the life and progress of the cruise. You can see all that is on the horizon; hear all the signals that are coming in, with warnings of typhoons ahead or of SOS messages from ships in trouble. Above all, you are made aware of the operational management and the demands of navigation as the liner progresses on its voyage. All this is uniquely fascinating and exciting as far as I am concerned.

'My ambition in life, therefore, has always been to be "on the bridge", whatever career I embarked on. I would hasten to add, however, that I was not so ambitious as to aspire to be captain, totally in charge. Rather, I wished to be alongside the people making the decisions, noting the course they were following. After much hard work, and a lot of faith and prayer into the bargain, I finally made it.'

During a brief spell in merchant banking in the early fifties Michael was elected to Kensington Borough Council and, by the early sixties, he was Depute Chairman of the North Kensington Conservative Association. His career at Westminster began when he was elected to Barkston Ash in 1964 at the age of 38. He has retained his seat at each election since then and is currently Member of Parliament for Selby (following boundary changes in 1983).

It would be true to say that, having achieved his ambition and reached 'the bridge', he has not been simply an interested observer of the command for, on many occasions, he has given advice on the direction the ship should take and, it must be added, has frequently had the ear of the captain, if not a hand on the wheel.

These opportunities came, for example, when he was Parliamentary Under Secretary of State at the Department of Health and Social Security; Minister of State for Northern Ireland and later at the Department of Employment. As Parliamentary Private Secretary to the Prime Minister, Margaret Thatcher, for four years from 1983, he was much closer to the side of the captain than even he aspired to in his youth.

Continuing with the maritime analogy, I put it to him that life on the bridge was surely frequently fraught with difficult decisions which the crew along with the captain had to make. How has he found himself reacting at the height of a crisis on the open sea of politics?

'I have to say that in over thirty years in the House I have rarely had agonising dilemmas which I could not resolve. Almost every decision I have had to make of a purely political kind I have been quite confident that it was the right one. More often than not, it has also been in accordance with what my party was prescribing. There have been many decisions of a moral and ethical kind, such as abortion, in-vitero fertilisation, capital punishment and issues to do with pornography, when I have had absolutely no doubt at all where my Christian imperatives directed me. In most of these areas, the party system made no claims on me at all; the whips were off, as they generally are for moral and social issues which affect the conscience.

'Furthermore, leaving aside for the moment such issues of conscience, the party whip is rather crudely misunderstood outside parliament. It is usually applied only when a consensus has emerged from the backbenchers as to what they will tolerate and accept when the vote is taken. Until the whips have taken soundings there is no point in applying the whip as they will simply ignore it. Governments set aside this principle at their peril, as Margaret Thatcher found in 1986 when she forced through a vote to try to change the Sunday trading laws.'

From a Christian standpoint, Michael believes that the reality of life in the House is such that there are very rarely clear cut decisions on secular or day to day political issues, when 'the Christian way' is unmistakeable. In support of his argument, he referred to the writings of a former Archbishop of Canterbury, William Temple:

There is no Christian solution to the problems presented by human self will but there is a cure for the self will and if you allow that cure to have effect then the problems are not solved, they are abolished.

'Temple goes on to give as an example the account in the Gospels of the two brothers who sought Jesus' help with their financial dispute, asking him, "Lord, will you decide and divide the inheritance between us?" Temple points out that they were asking the Lord to arbitrate between two self-centred claims so he refused to co-operate with them, saying, "Take heed and keep yourself from all covetousness." Temple concluded that, if they had taken that advice, they would not have had a problem.

'I find myself in accord with the archbishop - and indeed our Lord - on this matter as I feel that, broadly speaking, everything in politics is a species of arbitration between self-centred claims and there is no strictly applicable Christian solution in any of those areas. Invariably, it is a matter of choice between greater or lesser evils. The challenge for the Christian in politics is to work out which is indeed the lesser evil and to have the courage to vote accordingly.

'To give but one example, is it preferable in social policy affecting the need to reduce unwanted teenage pregnancies to have an intensive programme of sex education in schools, with no holds barred as to what is taught and with free contraceptives available; or is free and easy abortion a better alternative? I realise that this may sound too crude and simple an example but the problem remains that, whatever of these you choose, neither is ideal, nor are they Christian solutions. The biblical standpoint seems to be straightforward, if radical, in today's climate: it is abstinence and self denial. If, however, that line is not generally acceptable, what arises after that does not admit of a Christian solution.

'Therefore, if I had to choose in these circumstances I would have no alternative but to vote on the side of those who wish to improve sex education and make contraceptives more freely accessible. Abstention from the vote at such a time is to risk the greater evil taking place. It is very difficult, if one is in a decision making situation, when the Christian solution is seen as radical, non-applicable and generally not available. So we are always making judgements in face of a dilemma between non-ideal alternatives.

'Capital punishment is another example. It was once considered terribly arrogant for MPs to reject what seemed to be the call of the populace to bring back hanging at a time when the murder rate was increasing at a pace. I remember one occasion when I had to convince a constituent that I did not have my head in the clouds on this matter.

'One of the tabloids was running a huge campaign coinciding with the Conservative Party Conference to persuade us to vote in favour of reintroduction. The headline read, 89% POLL IN FAVOUR. The debate went on all morning with various well-known politicians of the day, experienced solicitors and others, persuasively putting forward their points of view. As all the concerns and ramifications were raised and aired, I became aware that it was as much an educational as a political experience. The protagonists in both camps had never fully considered the dilemmas and had to admit that the arguments were less black and white than they had at first appreciated.

'When the vote came out in favour by a very small

majority, it only served to reinforce my belief that there are indeed grey areas to measure up. I was able to tell my constituent that, at the end of the day, that is what I am called to do as an MP, particularly when there is no clear cut answer or unequivocal advice given. I am no different from many others in a variety of different callings and professions; it is just that, in my position, I regularly have to make decisions which are much more finely balanced than the man in the street imagines the situation to be. Perhaps this is why politicians often seem to be out of step with the opinions of many of their constituents.

'Some of my colleagues have proposed referendums, rather than polls, as a way to identify the wishes of the majority in certain circumstances. But I have a problem here, believing that it is often extremely difficult for the population of a country to be emotionally detached on some issues. This method of gathering opinions may exploit ignorances and prejudices rather than lead the way in the light of knowledge and evidence. There is little doubt that hanging would have been restored by popular demand in this country a long time ago but we are aware now that there would have been several irrevocable mis-carriages of justice in murder trials in recent years.'

When I discussed with Michael the place that party politics has in his thinking I wondered whether it was easier or more difficult to be a Christian as a Conservative than it may be in another camp. He made no attempt to skirt round this difficult question but explained clearly why he believes his brand of politics offers some an-swers, but not all the solutions, to the challenges of today's world.

'I hold to the argument that the Conservative belief in the freedom of the individual is closest to the Christian analysis of the nature of man. The human being is made in the image of God and is individually, personally, loved and redeemed through the death of Christ on the cross. That person has an over-riding significance as an individual in God's sight and no man or woman can be seen as subordinate to the state or serving the purposes of the state. The state must always be subordinate to the individual, serving his or her needs. One of the characteristics of the individual is that human personality is developed partly through being in contact with others in society. Humans are inescapably social, even if initially only within the context of the family but, increasingly as a child grows up, his personality is determined by choice between alternative options and courses.

'The exercise of choice by the individual is a crucial feature of my political philosophy and the intervention by the state in the pursuit of social or collective ends which might mean the restriction, limitation or over-riding of freedom to choose, is a tendency which I would expect to find much less in the Conservative party and much more in the Labour party, for example.'

I put it to him that many believe that members of the early church claimed to follow the example of Christ by their caring for and sharing with others in a collective, some would say socialist, way among the people of their time. Should this not be the guide for Christians today? Starting off with others in mind rather than ourselves as individuals? He was clear in his viewpoint.

'It is true that the early church manifested a form of

communalism, in that they had all things in common, which is perhaps closer to the socialist vision. No person thought of that which they owned belonging to themselves. I turn again to the writings of William Temple who analysed that early society. I find myself agreeing with his belief that the essence of the situation was freedom and voluntary renunciation of property. There is no evidence that there was constraint laid on any members of the early church who placed their goods and assets at the disposal of the apostles.

'Even when we consider the case of Ananias and Sapphira, who suffered the consequences of cheating their fellow believers, Peter said to them, "You were not under any obligation to hand over your property and your fault was not that you held it back but that you pretended to do otherwise." So it was their deceit, their hypocrisy which condemned them, not their failure to give to the common good. That lends itself rather awkwardly to programmes of compulsory redistribution and levies of large personal taxation. This, I believe, is more coercive than Christian and can limit and detract from human freedom in a way which causes people to suffer more than they might otherwise. I therefore think that any connection between socialism and early Christian thinking is tenuous, to say the least.

'I believe that the aim of our party to build on the family and small units of organisation, while allowing for the rights of the individual, is the way forward. In a complicated society such as ours there are, of course, situations where the state has to take the lead to ensure fair distribution of resources but it is the extent of state interference which divides us from other parties. I do accept that there are Christians in those parties who are honest in their own opposing beliefs and I respect them for the stand that they take.'

Expanding on the aim to build up the family and sustain the values which that represents as a basis for society today, we discussed how political programmes can strengthen this.

'There are many programmes in government social spending which aim to support family life but I would not pretend that these are unique to the Conservative party. This is one of the areas of common ground which attracts endorsement by all parties in recognition of such a central pillar in our society today. Any differences are to do with the level of funding and the degree of intervention. The party in government is no less aware of the needs but has the tricky problem of having to raise the money. Parties in opposition have more freedom to "window shop" and make recommendations based on what they would like to see done without the responsibility of supplying the wherewithal to carry them out!'

If the party of government finds it more difficult to be altruistic in the policies it pursues, I raised the possibility of this being a particular dilemma for a Christian MP in the party which is in power. To what extent is it easier to stand up for one's beliefs if one is in opposition?

'To a certain extent it is easier because, in opposition, one can advocate increased expenditure to help one section of society or another for very strong social reasons. For example, the scourge of unemployment weighs heavily on the conscience of all MPs and even more so if their constituents are affected. But the economic decisions which would allow any alleviation of the problem are harder to reach if one has to make cuts elsewhere to allow for it. Like it or not, even among Christians, this is often where differences of opinion will always be with us.

'Despite political wranglings which go on between ourselves and the opposition parties, there is common ground, and not uniquely among Christian MPs, that we should do our best to improve housing in terms of access and quality; to support children and elderly people, through good local authority provision; and to provide and encourage good education.

'As a Christian I feel particularly strongly that religious education should be strengthened in all schools, not only in the independent and denominational sectors. As far as I know, my Christian colleagues in all parties are united in this and we have been very active in lobbying for it. Not only is RE now accepted as a compulsory part of the curriculum, but also it is taken that it should be mainly Christian in content. While comparative religions, in a multi-faith society such as Britain now is, must also be recognised, I am not alone in believing that we have failed our children by allowing the teaching of basic Bible principles and the tenets of the Christian faith to be neglected. No other major world religion directly associated with a country has allowed this to happen.'

We talked about the future of society as we move rapidly to the turn of the century and discussed issues at the forefront of debate in politics which may be particularly challenging to Christian MPs. Among them was the development of broadcasting, not only the problem of ensuring that there is control over what can be sent out over the airwaves but also how to protect children in particular from harmful violence and pornography.

'That will always be a thorny issue, as we are seen as censors and inhibitors of free speech by a very vociferous lobby of people who frequently are part of multi-million pound empires with international connections. Even the most liberal of thinkers recognise that society must be protected from extreme and unnatural output via the media.

'But it should not always be negative. Many of us would like to see greater freedom for churches to broadcast and more opportunities for direct evangelism on public programmes and on the non-specialist channels. We would also like to see the strengthening of religious education in schools and the media can play its part here too.'

Also in Michael's vision for change towards 2000 is the cultivation of good housing, particularly for renting, to enable more young people to start in homes they can afford. He was also clear in his view that most Christians looking at the Sunday trading laws would believe that, given the alternatives between total deregulation (a complete free for all) and some sort of restriction and limitation on opening, would want to come down firmly on the latter.

'Advocate as I am of the recognition of the Christian Sunday, I believe that this is not purely a religious issue. There is what one might call "the rhythm of life argument" which applies to those of all faiths or none, that everyone needs a break, a time for recreation, physically as well as spiritually. This should be enforced by law, I believe, as there is no doubt in my mind that the removal of this basic right will undermine many aspects of social and family life in our country.'

In common with many other MPs, Michael Alison leads a rather hectic life. When we met together in his office at the far end of the Palace of Westminster, in the shadow of Big Ben, the phone rang constantly in competition with the division bell. As he talked about his timetable for the day, I couldn't help but notice the camp bed in the corner of the room and wondered if he ever had time to go home.

'It is indeed a very busy life and I do use the little bed here to rest from time to time, particularly during all night sittings. But I ensure that I go home to be with my family, even if not as frequently as they would like. I have three grown up children: Sebastian, Mary and James. I also have two granddaughters whom I love to be with whenever I can.

'Knowing when to take time to relax is vital, if difficult at times, and I appreciate the opportunity to take part in long distance running, which I find physically and mentally stimulating.

'Work in a Christian sphere is, of course, of central importance in my life. The devotional meetings of the Parliamentary Christian Fellowship and the privilege of having fellowship with other MPs are of great encouragement to me. Outside the House, I am involved in my local church and was, until recently, church warden of Holy Trinity Church in Brompton. I am currently Second Church Estates Commissioner, which is, in effect, Church of England Spokesman in the House of Commons.'

Michael Alison's political commitment is clear and unequivocal: with his 'view from the bridge', he knows the direction he wishes the parliamentary ship to follow. When it comes to the more important issues of a spiritual nature he is equally sure about the path he should take and, above all, he knows the Captain on the bridge. His Christian life and witness are testimony to that.

3

ANDREW WELSH
Scottish National Party MP for Angus East

Sweeping Away the Dust of Centuries

He put his key into the ignition and lifted the car phone to speak to his secretary. 'Hello, Sandra. Andrew here. The plane was a bit late so it will be after five before I get to the office. I promised Sheena that I would do my best to be home early tonight. Is there a lot of mail to attend to?'

'There are a few odds and ends for you to deal with and there are more letters about the abortion vote next week. You might want to take time to look at them over the weekend,' she replied.

'Yes I'll do that, if you could have them ready for me. See you later.'

He put the phone down and drove out of the airport. Had he been able to avoid joining the rush hour commuters making their way out of Edinburgh the trip home to Arbroath would have been much quicker. Although he was tired at the end of a busy week at Westminster the drive north gave him time to think and plan the next few days. But it was the mailbag on abortion which was uppermost in his mind that evening as he jostled with his fellow travellers in the usual traffic jams at that time of day.

Later he began to read over the many letters he had

received on the abortion issue. Each put up a case in support of one viewpoint or another. They ranged from the extreme of abortion on demand to total opposition to the practice, whatever the social or medical arguments put forward. Just as his thinking would be swayed by a heart-rending story from a victim of rape, he would read another from a young nurse faced with the sad reality of assisting at a clinic.

Thirty odd years ago, if anyone had suggested to young Andrew Welsh that his enthusiasm for Scottish Nationalism would lead him to claim a seat at Westminster he would have been flattered. Propose to him that he would one day be grappling with matters of conscience such as a vote on abortion and he might have laughed, perhaps muttering, 'What's that got to do with freedom for Scotland?' To a twelve year old, barely out of short trousers, such issues were probably not in his vocabulary far less on his 'agenda'.

Today the dream of an independent Scotland is never far from his mind and much of his energy as Member of Parliament for Angus East is expended on achieving that goal. He is also aware that as an elected representative there is other national and international business, not all directly related to Scotland, which demands his consideration as a politician.

Many decisions are clear cut and reflect the party's election manifesto but all too frequently there are matters of conscience and belief which exercise his mind and keep him awake at night. While it is a dilemma which all politicians face at some time or another, it is especially challenging for a Christian MP and Andrew Welsh ac-

knowledges that he cannot lightly ignore his background
and commitment to particular values and beliefs.

His interest and involvement in Scottish politics were
maintained throughout his school days at Govan High
School, on the south side of Glasgow, but he was persuaded to follow in his father's footsteps and embark on
a career in banking. However, when he started to work for
one of the Scottish banks, he did not relish the prospect of
earning a living this way until retirement. In addition, he
was keen to further his general education so set his sights
on obtaining entrance qualifications to Glasgow University.

After many long evenings of study as a mature student
he succeeded and finally graduated with honours in Modern History and Politics. Further post-graduate study
earned him a higher degree to allow him to embark on a
teaching career.

'I can barely remember a time when I was not interested in politics,' he recounted. 'Influenced at first by my
sister, I was fired by Scottish Nationalism and joined the
party at the age of twelve - illegally, in fact, as you had to
be at least sixteen! By the age of sixteen I was helping to
form branches in the city. I even managed to persuade my
father to become treasurer in our local branch. This was
quite a step for a respectable banker, as the SNP had more
of a reputation for being on the fringe of politics than it
has now.'

In the late fifties and early sixties many Scottish
families despaired of their prospects and emigrated to
Canada or Australia where most of them prospered. He
toyed with the idea of going abroad too but decided that

he would stay at home to fight for improved conditions within politics. The late Arthur Donaldson, who clearly and honestly expounded the basic principles of nationalism, had a great influence on his thinking. As an avid reader, he also studied the subject and came to the conclusion that Scotland had experienced prosperity in the past, that many Scottish men and women had led the world through their inventiveness and business acumen; so why not again today?

The Scottish National Party seemed to him to offer a way forward through the vision of a Scottish parliament where the electorate could find a voice, further their interests and prosper as other small countries in Europe were already doing.

'When people ask me why I am a Nationalist, I have to say that it is because I feel ashamed of the poverty and waste of talent which I see around a country which is rich in material and human resources. However, I would wish to stress that I have no truck for bigots whose anti-English rhetoric does not reflect the basic principles I speak of. I am not "anti" anyone, simply pro-Scottish in my outlook.'

He rose through the ranks and became an election agent at the age of nineteen. By his twenty-first birthday he was a local government candidate for the party and rubbed shoulders with prominent activists of his time. In the early seventies, while teaching at Stirling High School, he was elected to the District Council. This only whetted his appetite and he stood as parliamentary candidate for South Angus where he was elected in 1974 at the age of thirty.

He recalled that moment when he entered the magnificent Palace of Westminster for the first time to proudly take his seat in the House of Commons.

'I suppose every MP remembers the first occasion when they walked into the majestic lobby, wondering if the policeman on duty would know who they were. And it certainly was an occasion for myself, my family and my party; exciting yet challenging as I considered the responsibility I was taking on my shoulders.'

The young MP was given the positions of SNP Parliamentary Spokesman on Housing, Agriculture and the Self-employed and Small Businesses. In 1977 he became party whip.

By all accounts it seemed that Andrew Welsh ate, drank and slept politics and that anyone meeting him would be faced with a barrage of political rhetoric at all times. While there is no denying his faithfulness to the party and his commitment to Scotland, there is another dimension to the personality who stands up for his minority political opinions on the floor of the House of Commons. As a committed Christian, he is fired also by a belief in standards and values also under threat in today's world.

Brought up in a Christian home, he learned about the Bible and Christian things from his mother's knee. With his family he was a regular attender at worship in Fairfield Church, Glasgow.

'The Christian life was the normal way of life in our home and I do not recall one dramatic event, flash of inspiration or conversion experience as some would have it. Of course I knew about commitment to Christ and belief in Him and there was a time, perhaps when I joined the church as a teenager, that I became convinced that this was the life I wished to follow.

'If I was inspired by anyone in these formative years it was by the Rev. Kenneth Stewart whose sermons to the workers gathered in the sheds in Fairfields shipyard, drew the attention of many of the earthiest and hardest of men you would find anywhere. He was a fearless preacher who was not ashamed to raise the standard of Christ in his time. The basic and simple truths of the Bible which he expounded rang true with me as they did to many of his parishioners. I can still remember many of his words to this day.

'As chaplain to the yard he was a man of deeds as well as words when he met them face to face as they went about their daily tasks. I suppose I was inspired by his zeal in that area too, even when he confessed that not everyone was open to hear the message he had to deliver.

'I have learned in particular that, in evangelism as in politics, it is possible to come on so strong that people are put off the whole business. We have to go to people where they are and accept them for who they are when we meet them. Only then can we, with God's help, take them on to where they will find a more meaningful way of life. More often than not it is by our *being* as well as *doing* that others see the life that Christ has to offer. Sadly it seems that many Christians are afraid to stand up for what they believe.

'Without giving undue publicity to Islamic funda-mentalism, we need only look at the stand many Muslims are prepared to take in their day-to-day life to feel ashamed at times. When I was a student I worked as a bus conductor and recall one of my Pakistani drivers going briefly to the back of the bus to pray to Mecca. Saying grace before meals, regular worship and family prayers are examples of practices which many Christians have discontinued in a hectic, materialistic world. We are either afraid or ashamed to witness in this way or too caught up in our busy lives to take the time. There will never be a time when the message is not appropriate for today's living but I do not believe that preaching alone is the answer.'

To further illustrate his point he referred to the time when he moved to Arbroath, a town with many churches. With so many fine places of worship to attend with his wife and daughter it was not easy to choose.

'In my position I have had to attend more funerals than I would care to count. Ministers tend to read passages from the Bible which are tremendous in their power, with reference in particular to the resurrection. It is easy to go over the heads of the congregation, not all of whom will be regular churchgoers. For the message to be real today we have to remove the dust of centuries and avoid the jargon which may be an impediment to understanding in modern society. The minister then of St. Andrew's Church in Arbroath, the Rev. Ian MacLeod, did just that at a funeral I had to attend. I was greatly moved by the experience and felt that this was the congregation we should join.'

Now an elder there he takes part in as many activities as travel between Westminster and home will permit; one of the disadvantages of being an MP for a constituency far from London. He enjoys also the fellowship of the prayer breakfasts which take place from time to time in his area and in London. These interdenominational gatherings, supported by clergy and laymen alike, are tremendously popular in many parts of Britain with little or no publicity surrounding them. They are not organised to be like a church service and their informality is the attraction for many who may not otherwise attend.

'I believe that these gatherings meet a need which is not being fulfilled by many established churches. They provide an opportunity for people to come together for worship to express themselves as they feel appropriate. Some are more extrovert than others but if it is not domineering it does not matter as long as the worship is heavenward! The clergy do not dominate and it is for them also to find fellowship and be refreshed as they meet together with fellow believers.'

In 1979, after five years fighting for his constituency and his party at Westminster, there was a general election and Andrew experienced the trauma of losing his seat - by only 700 votes! His political career was not at an end by any means but he had to earn his living. After a short spell in teaching he took up a post as lecturer in Economics and Politics at the former Dundee College of Commerce. A short time later he became senior lecturer in Business Administration at Angus College of Further Education.

Remaining active in local politics he was elected provost of Angus District Council in 1984 and, at the general election in 1987, found himself again at Westminster. He was returned as party whip and since then has been involved in a number of committees including the

Select Committee on Members Interests and the Select
Committee on Scottish Affairs.

The responsibility which he has to represent his party
and the people of Angus East is never far from his mind,
whatever the post he holds or voice he wishes to raise in
the House.   There are many things he would like to see
happen and changes he longs to see effected but there is
the constant frustration of being one of a minority party
sitting on the side of the opposition against an established
government.

'It would be simple for politicians to say that they will
guarantee the earth to their constituents when they address the faithful or speak at a public rally but I feel that
I would be unfaithful to my own conscience if I did so. I
do my best to be available on the phone, to answer letters
and to meet people face to face.

'At my surgeries when people seek my help I promise
to do my best and dedicate as much time as possible to
their case; to ignore them would be wrong but to raise
false hopes would be unscrupulous. Politics has a bad
name these days and one thing I know I must do is show
honesty and integrity in all matters.'

In the melee of the House of Commons, when point
scoring is the order of the day, he finds that to maintain
this public image is easier said than done. Like attracts
like in politics and it would be easier to surround himself
with people who agree with him and look out only for
allies to support the cause.

'If one wishes to be a true representative of the people
the organisation must be such that it reflects the will of the
electorate as a whole, as far as is humanly possible. More

often than not I find myself exploring the intersection of various interests. This is particularly so in a party like ours which claims to cover a wide spectrum of political opinion albeit with one common nationalist goal.

'If I ever forget that I am the servant of the people, not their master, I will be failing in my duty as an MP and a Christian. My aim is to be able to say that I have served my community well and with honesty and commitment. People may vote against me for my political beliefs - this is democracy - but I trust that I will always be able to hold my head high as I walk down the street in my home town. Much of politics has been tainted by the failure of representatives of the people to adhere to this basic principle.'

It was the conviction that he had so much 'unfinished business' to attend to that drove him to seek re-election rather than pursue a more secure career outside politics. Much of his time is taken up with wider issues related to the various committees he participates in. As party whip there are occasions when he has to 'toe the party line' but there are times for all MPs when individual belief and conscience must take precedence. There is an opt-out clause which he can refer to if matters conflict with personal or constituency interests. On most contentious areas his group are generally able to reach a consensus.

'On a free vote in the House of Commons, when it is down to individual belief, the most difficult I have ever had to consider followed the debate on abortion. I have always maintained that it is important to distinguish between political and moral issues but frequently the line between them is blurred. Where it is a manifesto matter, my opinion will reflect that but, when it comes to certain moral

issues, I must question whether I have the right to force my
views on others if they are out of line with the majority. I
must therefore consult while reserving the right to cast my
vote on issues of extreme conscience.'

He consults different groups in the community, such
as farmers or industrialists, and invites members of the
clergy from all denominations to meet him and to raise
areas of concern to them. On the issue of abortion, he
consulted nurses, doctors, social workers and the clergy.
He aims not only to try to reflect their views as their
representative, but also to seek clarification and guidance
for his own benefit on matters which may cause him
concern, as a Christian and an MP. They may not all agree
with the line he takes but it permits constructive dialogue
and can make them more aware of the challenges he must
face when the chips are down and a vote is called for in the
House.

'Even among Christians, there are differing arguments, each as cogent as the other, and I am aware that,
whatever way I vote, I may have offended someone. With
varying points of view spinning around inside my head,
I am not ashamed to confess that there are times when I
pray to ask what I should do and say in the circumstances.

'After much consultation, heart-searching and prayer
I found myself rejecting the two extremes on the issue of
abortion. I was then faced with the difficulty of drawing
a line between them to arrive at a decision which, above
all, I could live with. I admit that I am still plagued with
conflicting thoughts on the matter and it will remain for
me one of the most difficult debates in which I have been
called upon to participate.

'Just as challenging are the ethical arguments of certain aspects of embryology. The problem is that, as technology is forging ahead, so are medical and surgical skills progressing to such an extent that many techniques can be carried out today that seemed impossible only a short time ago. Society is riven by moral and political contention.

'While we may marvel at the benefits which progress can bring to society, I have this feeling that morality has not kept pace with such developments. People from all walks of life look for a moral lead as science collates data and moves forward in leaps and bounds into a world with as many questions as answers. This is where the church and Christian people can offer guidance and support, for these are issues which, more often than not, go above and beyond politics. Having said that, it is frequently left to parliament to draw boundaries and set guidelines. That is the seat of my dilemma.'

The role of the church in politics is as controversial a debate today as it has ever been. Andrew Welsh would maintain that the church must be involved in life. As political decisions are part of life, it follows, therefore, that no Christian can stand on the sidelines without raising a voice, particularly if the poor are seen to suffer.

'Having said that, it is the job of the church to proclaim eternal truths and it must interpret them in a way which reflects the circumstances of the age and meets the needs of each generation. The church has a moral duty to speak up, but if the debate begins to degenerate into party politics, that can be a problem. When I was a member of the Church and Nation Committee (a Church of Scotland committee), party politics did not come into the discussion as we looked at each issue on its own merit and, most importantly, in the light of Scripture. If this is the basis of debate it is more likely that wise council will lead to a clear viewpoint emerging which can be conveyed to the decision makers.'

The other side of the coin, he believes, is that politicians are in danger of using religion to further their own ends. Christians in politics could well see one stance or another as being a vote winner in a particular situation. He gave me an illustration from his own experience.

'When chairman of the prayer breakfasts, I was very sensitive to the fact that some might think that my participation was just another way to attract a sector of the voting population to my party. My Christian life and witness is intertwined with my political life in many respects, but Christ did not belong to a political party and there is no biblical precedence for voting one way or another at an election. Even if we hold to the view that ultimately the Bible can provide us with all the answers to our questions it is the nature of theological debate that there will continue to be points of contention. Didn't Paul say, "... for now we see through a glass darkly..." We must remember this and remain open to change or we will surely be giving credence to the "ayatollahs" of this world; offering obeyance to an "oracle" which claims to have the whole truth.

'At the same time it is important for Christian groups to take the initiative, meet with politicians of all viewpoints and put their case to them. This may help them to vote intelligently in the House or take issue with the government on a particular area of concern. There are Christians in all political parties and I would hope that these principles would inform and educate those whom I represent as much as any other.

'The Christian message is timeless and very powerful. If we are able to remove the trappings, rid ourselves of the dust of centuries that I spoke of earlier, we can uncover the fundamental truths of the gospel. Then I am sure we can deliver a message which will strike a chord with a society which has a crying need for spiritual direction.'

In the House of Commons he appreciates the support which Christian MPs give each other as they face seemingly insurmountable dilemmas from one week to the next. Notwithstanding the valuable opportunity to share common challenges, I wondered if there was a danger that this may become 'a house within a house', where party politics dominate yet again, and tactics and influences undermine matters of faith and belief? He was quite clear in his reply to me.

'No one party can claim to be more Christian than another but we can seek common spiritual goals. The House of Commons Christian Fellowship is one supportive way of doing this which I appreciate greatly. We may appear to fight tooth and nail in the chamber but are encouraged as we meet away from the floor of the Commons for fellowship and prayer.

'We know each other, and friendships go across party boundaries but we do not take advantage of this to score political points. One of the difficulties is that an MP's existence is so hectic that it is virtually impossible to find a time to meet which is convenient for all who may be interested to attend. When we do meet we would pray rather for wisdom in our deliberations than for particular outcomes, which may vary according to our political standpoint.

'To return to the influence of groups, it is worth remembering that they can also play an important supportive role and learn to appreciate the dilemmas which MPs may encounter. Some lobby their members on a host of concerns. While this is a legitimate and valuable part of the democratic process, it can take its toll on us. We are no less human than anyone else: Christians should pray for their MP and support as well as attack on particular issues. In this way we can help to ensure that there is a moral input into the debate across the political spectrum. Dealing with eternal values can bring the politician down to size.

'So often I wish to deal with a particular concern raised by a constituent and find that, even as an MP, my influence is limited when I find myself in debate with members of "quangos", who are nominated by the government, but seem accountable to nobody in the community. There is what I call "an arrogance of power" and it is important that those whom we elect never forget that they are elected to serve, not to rule, as I have said before. It has been argued that our present government has been in power so long that some may have forgotten this. However, in a democracy, the electorate have the ability to temper this if they so wish. We ignore this at our peril.'

There is always the danger that communities decide that every move an MP makes, or cause he supports, is nothing other than electioneering; vote gathering when it suits him. This is no less the case when he becomes involved in church activities. Andrew spoke of 'the Billy Graham dilemma', referring to the situation in the USA when presidents are keen to appear publicly with the evangelist whenever its seems politically expedient.

It can be hurtful if he feels that church groups or individuals try to 'hijack' him because he is an MP and his membership or support would afford them privileges, or appear to grant a status they might not otherwise have. It is hard to say 'no', yet impossible to support all worthy causes, or attend every meeting which boasts his name on its membership list. At times he feels that it is a form of moral blackmail, a 'no win' situation which he cannot honestly respond to for fear of further misunderstanding.

The life of an MP is hectic and travel up and down to London takes its toll on Andrew Welsh as much as it does on many of his colleagues. He also must remind himself that he represents all members of his constituency, all shades of opinion and belief, and that there are dangers in mixing leisure and recreation with politics.

'I cannot stress enough that, contrary to some people's opinion, my membership of a church, my position as an elder, my attendance at gatherings of Christians anywhere, have nothing to do with vote seeking nor a desire to raise the SNP banner in one more corner of the community: that would be a total abuse of my position. Rather it is about meeting for worship or seeking fellowship and spiritual recreation in my life. As I constantly give out to others I also need to be replenished spiritually and physically. The bottom line is that I wish to be influenced and strengthened as an MP by my faith and beliefs.'

That accepted, I wondered, nevertheless, whether he found himself praying or asking others to pray that he would be returned to parliament at each election.

'No, not in such a direct way. To ask God to give victory to a specific party would be wrong. I pray rather that my conduct as a candidate would be an advert for the faith I confess; that if elected I would be able to do things and act in a particular way. On the other hand I do not "hide my light under a bushel" and avoid including in my election address that I am a kirk elder, for example. To attempt to win votes by appearing neutral in these matters would also be dishonest.'

At the end of a busy week in politics, Andrew values the opportunity to relax with his wife Sheena, a learning support teacher in Arbroath Academy and their teenage daughter Jane. Family life is important to him and he is aware that the pressures of politics can lead to neglect of these valuable relationships. Meetings, phone calls and many other demands on his time can interrupt at the most inopportune moment.

As he humorously put it, 'I sometimes felt that I was part of the dirty washing that comes home on Fridays from London and the clean washing that flies down to Heathrow on Mondays.' He was quick to point out, however, that he now does his own washing in his London flat so this is no longer an appropriate analogy!

'If I had my family with me in London I could be home every night but that is the price I have to pay for being an MP who wishes to live in his constituency. My wife is the mainstay, the one who keeps things going on the home front in Scotland.

'After a recent illness I am also aware that I must take time to relax and unwind for the sake of my family and to maintain my effectiveness as an MP; the lifestyle in the House of Commons is bizarre, to say the least, with the strangest of hours for meetings and debates. In no way is the life conducive to relaxation or supportive of the demands of home and family. If "burnout" takes place I am no use to anyone. God expects us to look after and care for what we have been blessed with - our relationships and the bodies we live in!'

Politicians are at the forefront of the debate about the erosion of family values.   Statistics on divorce, child abuse etc. are never far from the headlines, particularly if an extreme case captures the imagination of the media. What particular contribution can the Christian MP make to the discussion?

'It is a situation which confronts every profession. In a class of pupils today, every teacher is aware that single parent families are all too common. And social workers have to deal with it at the sharp end also. It would be all too easy to pontificate and ignore the real hurt that individuals experience but I believe that the family must be the foundation stone of our society and clearly this is the basis of Christian belief also.

'This is where the church can come in by making these values meaningful in people's lives. Historically, the state may have unwittingly helped to undermine the role which the church once had in this sphere of life, by creating social structures which suggest that we do not need to care for our neighbour as we once did. If people saw that Christianity was for living every day of the week and the church not just the provider of the "God slot" on a Sunday, things might improve in society. It is for those in the pews on a Sunday to reach out with the message by their life and example for the rest of the week. I do not mean ramming the gospel down people's throats but rather by being the "salt" that Christ spoke of.

'Without denying the crucial role of the church here, I would be wrong to ignore the part that political decisions can have on people's lives. It has been shown that economic difficulties are the cause of breakdown in some families and it cannot be denied that the scourge of unemployment affects lives. When I left school, jobs were plentiful but today, no matter how well qualified a young person may be, there is no guarantee of employment. I would be foolish as an MP and a Christian if I denied the effect this must have on the morale of individuals and on family life. Politicians can have an influence on social and economic decisions.

'We should embrace the idea of community rather than promote the supremacy of the individual as some politicians would have us do. Of course I believe in the rights of the individual but this does not extend to his right to trample on others in society to gain advantage over them. In one sense I do not care how rich a person becomes, if their wealth is honestly gained, but I do care compassionately how poor a person is. I believe that there are certain standards below which no individual or family should be allowed to fall. The proper distribution of a country's wealth is something the politician can speak out on.'

In today's world, 'nationalism' has been tainted by

scenes of war and conflict in many corners of the globe. To openly propose it as a way to promote the wellbeing of a nation is to be misunderstood in many political circles in Britain but the Scottish National Party holds firm to its beliefs and is not afraid to share its vision with the electorate north and south of the Border. Andrew shared with me the vision that he has as an MP in his party and why he believes that achieving this particular political goal will benefit his country, from a Christian standpoint.

'Nationalism can mean anything from the heroic stance of William Tell to the leadership of Winston Churchill; or the fanaticism of Adolf Hitler to the tyranny of Idi Amin, the discredited Ugandan despot. Any "ism", if taken to extreme, can challenge belief and be an abuse of power. I am Scottish and I care for the future of my country. We have grown used to poverty in many parts of our land despite the vast wealth of material and human resources available to us. As a nationalist and a Christian I cannot help but raise a voice of concern over circumstances which have led people to despair and feel that their self respect has been undermined.

'Scotland has long been proud of its institutions; these include the church and legal and education systems. We have an executive in Scottish Office ministers but we lack a legislature to allow us to make our own decisions to oversee the work done by them. Smaller countries than ours in Europe already have that. At the moment we have neither a voice, a vote nor a veto in Europe except through London.

'I realise that I am on a soapbox again and you might ask why I believe things may improve spiritually in

Scotland if it had a greater say in its own affairs. Traditionally, Scotland has shared its knowledge and wealth with the world. Inventors, business leaders and missionaries have gone out in larger numbers per head of population than from any other nation.

'Down through the ages the church in Scotland has had a central role in sustaining a sense of fairness, egality and social justice within our society. Education is a prime example of this. In the eighteenth century there were only two national education systems in the world; in China and in Scotland. In China it was very élitist; in Scotland it was a great example of egalitarianism: the son of the landowner sat at the same school desk as the crofter's child.

'I humbly believe that Scotland would have the opportunity to return to these values and standards if it were able as a nation to set its own agenda.'

Having said that, Andrew expressed his concern that Christianity might be abused by politicians if it is used for selfish political ends. While there is no denying his commitment to nationalism in Scotland he stressed again and again that his is only one of many voices contributing to the great debate.

4
MARTIN SMYTH
Ulster Unionist MP for Belfast South

Pulpit Exchange

It happened very early one Sunday morning in July 1970.
The Reverend Martin Smyth and his family had gone to
bed in preparation for a busy day of services, two in his
own congregation and one in County Down some thirty
miles away. He was sleeping soundly, as usual, until a
strange sensation awoke him. An explosion had rocked
the building.

'What's the matter?' Martin murmured sleepily to his
wife Kathleen, who was already awake.

'It's a bomb!' she replied.

'Where?' he asked.

'In our front room, by the sound of it,' she responded.

Immediately Martin was out of bed and into the room
where his two daughters were in a state of shock. Thank-
fully, none on them was hurt but it was a sharp reminder,
if they needed it, that no one was immune from the
troubles that were engulfing Northern Ireland.

Their first caller, minutes after the explosion, was a
journalist who claimed he had heard the address on the
police radio wavelength. Like others, Martin often wondered at how much collusion there was between some
reporters and terrorist organisations. He also marvelled at

the inane questions they posed in such tragic circumstances. On this occasion, the reporter asked, 'Who do
you think it was?' and was startled with Martin's answer:
'Some kind friend sending an endearing message!'

'My curt reply was not simply an attempt to be humorous in the heat of the moment,' Martin explained, ' I feel
strongly that anyone who plants a bomb must be held
responsible for their actions. Terrorists are often reported
as "apologising", with some hypocrisy, because they had
hit the wrong target. To set a bomb at a manse door could
have maimed or murdered anyone. Even through the night
people can visit a manse for help or the minister could be
going out in response to a call. If we had not taken some
care, our eldest daughter could have been killed that night,
as she normally slept in the room above the front entrance
where the bomb was placed.'

Ten years later, by agreeing to accept the nomination
to stand for election as Ulster Unionist Member of Parliament for Belfast South, Martin Smyth knew only too well
that he would not only be caught in the crossfire of debate
at Westminster but that he would also be in the firing line
of the terrorists. The life of his predecessor in the seat had
been tragically cut short by an assassin's bullet. When he
accepted the invitation to take his place he did not need to
be told that he would be subjected to round the clock
security, perhaps for the rest of his life.

All politicians are conscious of the need for vigilance
but it is a way of life which only the dedicated in Northern
Ireland choose to follow. As an ordained Presbyterian
minister, Martin could have remained a pastor to his
congregation, have continued to preach regularly from

the pulpit and left the solving of the constitutional problems to the politicians. There was a time when he was sorely tempted to do so even though he was actively involved in the local party. But events overtook him and he soon became aware that God was calling him to serve in this way.

'When I look back on my life,' he continued, 'I suppose I could have gone in a different direction but for the intervention of God. Whatever the plans of my parents, or the vision I had for my own future, when I dedicated my life to God I should have realised that His plans would supersede everything else.   The alternative road may have looked more attractive but I knew that I could only be happy if I followed the direction that He wanted me to go. I cannot deny that it is a risky path to take, particularly when I am regularly subjected to a tight cordon of security, have telephoned threats and even bombings but I have a peace in my heart that this is what God wants me to do.'

If there is such a thing as an 'ordinary' politician, Martin Smyth certainly is not one of them. To understand what has shaped his political and religious thinking we have to go back to his childhood in Northern Ireland.

He and his twin brother Crawford were born in 1931 in a terraced house on the Donegal Road in the heart of the city of Belfast. It was a working class home where every penny had to be counted, particularly when the breadwinner was forced out of work for a lengthy period with pleurisy, a symptom of the gas attacks he had to endure in the trenches during the First World War. These were days when there was no National Health Service to pick up the cost of medicines and the grocer's bill had to be set against the doctor's account when trying to balance the family budget.

He described his parents as being 'nominal Christians' as they attended church from time to time but were not communicant members. It would be years later, when Martin was ordained, that they would become more committed. Nevertheless, they made sure that he and his brother went regularly to Sunday School and in all respects their life of dedication to their family were shining examples which he has never forgotten.

War broke out during his early education at Donegal Road Methodist Primary School, affectionately known in the area as 'Tintop', because of its corrugated iron roof. Along with many other city children he and his brother were evacuated to the relative quiet of Fermanagh to the home of a couple with no children. Wishing to do their bit for the war effort they were delighted to offer shelter to the attractive twins, not realising what they were taking on!

'With no family of their own,' Martin recalled, 'the McClures should have known better than to take on the Smyth twins. We got up to all sorts of mischief, as my parents could have warned them. After a month or so we moved to be with the Wilsons who had an only son, Aubrey. They were very kind to us. We were sent to a wee two teacher school, Jones Memorial, which was a sharp contrast to the city primary we were used to. There were two hard working members of staff who gave us an excellent basic education which proved to be a good start for us.

'Mr and Mrs Wilson were a dedicated Christian couple and we were well churched, attending at least two Sunday services plus Sunday School! Although we were rather weary at times at the end of the day, we didn't think much about it. It was something we had to do and, in retrospect, it gave us a good grounding in the Christian faith which we might not otherwise have had.'

Despite the continuing danger, it was decided that the boys should return to Belfast to take up their secondary education at the Methodist College, a co-educational grammar school in the city. Crawford later left school to go into business, but Martin remained to obtain further qualifications to allow him to go on to higher education.

During this period, he became more and more interested in Christian things and not simply out of habit as he continued to attend church regularly. He recalls being influenced by one Sunday School teacher in particular.

'Her name was Eva Craig. She spoke in a very simple and direct way to us, I remember, but it was her life and example, as much as her words, which made a lasting impression on those who attended her classes. So great was her influence that many continued to go to her group as adults to benefit from her teaching. I still remember as a young fellow saying, "Lord if I'm good to the end of the year I'll be better next year!", feeling that I wanted to follow her example. I grew up to respect the Bible, the Lord's Day and all that the church stood for but, above all, I came to realise that Christians were not simply those who lived a good life but were people who had put their faith in Christ for forgiveness of sins and to enable them to live for Him. I did not have a dramatic experience at a church service, it was just an acknowledgement of Him as my Saviour and Lord during my life at home.'

As a boy, even before he had made a commitment to church membership, when asked the usual question about what he wanted to do when he grew up, more often than not he said that he wanted to be a clergyman. To this day in the family album there is a photograph of Martin and his twin brother in fancy dress. Crawford is dressed as a red Indian while Martin is wearing the garb of a minister.

'For a number of years, I began to think that I would be taking another path, not because of a change of heart, but because I had serious doubts whether I could make the grade educationally. When my brother left school I soldiered on and promised God that, if I got good results, I would fulfil my original intention and go in for the ministry. As time went by, it seemed that I would not get there as I needed greater success with languages but I succeeded and applied to Magee University, a Presbyterian foundation in Londonderry associated with Trinity College, Dublin. That was 1949.'

His application to Magee was successful, but as the university was not government funded, Martin did not receive a scholarship to attend. His parents helped him as much as they could and he supplemented this by working in the office of Ulster Transport during the long summer holidays.

At university he was helped greatly by the opportunity for discussion within the Evangelical Union and the Inter Varsity Fellowship, particularly as he grappled with many of the confusing theological debates of the day. Much of the liberal theology conflicted with the teaching

he had received in his youth. It could have been a traumatic time of doubt for him had he not been able to debate
the wider issues and take account of the evangelical
standpoint.

'It is often argued that evangelical theology is intoler-
ant of other viewpoints but I found, in my training, the
most illiberal stance was in fact taken by liberal theologians who refused to recognise any opinion not in accord
with their beliefs.'

He graduated from Trinity College, Dublin in 1953
before taking a postgraduate course at the Assembly's
College, Belfast, where the theological conflicts were no
less controversial. The key difference, he recalls, was
that there was a respect for individual beliefs, as far as
assignments and examinations were concerned, as long
as the content of the argument was reasoned and soundly
based on text.

While at college he was student assistant at Finaghy
and had the opportunity to experience a wide range of
pastoral work in different communities. When he was
finally licensed in 1955, he had made up his mind that he
would not apply for a charge but would wait until a
congregation invited him.

'At college I had learned to trust in God to provide for
my every need, financially and otherwise, but it was still
difficult to take this on board as I was afraid that I might
end up where I didn't want to go. I asked for God's
guidance and the verse in my reading at the time was
*"There shall be no sign but that given to the prophet
Jonah ..."*. This was a clear reference to the cross and the
resurrection. I was not to keep looking for signs but to

obey God. I was not to make the mistake that Jonah made, even if I was asked to go as the minister to a congregation which may prove to be challenging and rewarding theologically and pastorally.'

He was called to a rural congregation of two hundred and fifty in an attractive little place called Raffrey, which Martin described as 'hardly a village, with only twenty five houses and a crossroads.' Despite some reservations about this being his first charge, he was encouraged to accept the call when he was made aware that the invitation had been unanimous. With his wife Kathleen, whom he had met during his student days and married just before he was ordained, he spent six challenging and very rewarding years there.

'These were exciting and encouraging times in our life. With God's help the congregation was strengthened and blessed, with many coming to know the Lord and joining our number. It was also a time of new beginnings for Kathleen and me, as our two children, Rosemary and Heather, were born to us during our years at Raffrey. We were really happy and felt that we would have willingly stayed there for many more years had it been in God's plan.

'When a call came for us to go to Alexandra in Belfast, we wrestled with it for a long time and I turned it down. Some time later I was asked to preach in Belfast so that the congregation could hear me. I told them that I did not believe that my expository style of ministry would suit them but they persisted and came along to hear me in my own church. When they later met and informed me that it was a unanimous call, once again I had to tell them that

God may have told them but He certainly hadn't put me in the picture!

'I did realise, however, that if I were being completely honest to God and with myself, I had not really been open to a call elsewhere as I was so happy in Raffrey that I did not want to leave. It was, after all, our first home together and the place where we had our children. Neither did my wife want to exchange a lovely rural setting for inner city Belfast. Above all, God was blessing us; surely a seal on the situation. We spent a long time in prayer about it and, as on previous occasions, God spoke to me through the Bible. My reading at that time was in Jeremiah and the verse: *Go prophesy to the North*, seemed to shout at me. Alexandra was certainly in the North Belfast Presbytery and that gave us more to think about!

'In the end we felt that it was God's will for us to go and we did so. It was a sad time also as we had to wrench ourselves away from the congregation who were disappointed that we had to move on at that point in our lives. Whereas I would have been happy to spend the rest of my days in Raffrey, I went to Belfast with the idea in mind that I would do up to twenty years and then be willing to step aside for a younger person to work in such a taxing and challenging location.

'If I needed it, the seal of the Lord on my call there came at the prayer of installation to the charge. I was weary and exhausted with the trauma of uprooting the family to our new home in Belfast but at that very moment I had such a sense of peace and strength. It must have been God's hand for I was certainly not feeling that way at the beginning of the evening.'

Martin served there for five years until 1968 when the outbreak of the present troubles took place in Northern Ireland. He had dabbled in politics earlier in his life, helping the Unionist Party from time to time during election campaigns. As a youngster he had been brought up in the Orange tradition, joining the local lodge with his brother.

'In those days, the Orange Order had close links with the churches. Meetings were held in an atmosphere of prayer and the Scriptures were read. Yes, there were marches and we upheld the Unionist traditions but I do not hold to the view that it reflected extreme Protestantism as the media portrays it today. Sadly the foundation of Christian principles with their associated constraints on behaviour have been eroded. Many Protestant young people feel that the church has failed to present a case for its people in Northern Ireland.'

The failure of the church to take a clear stand on certain issues was one of the reasons why Martin became involved in politics, first of all at branch level. His was an attempt to bridge the ever widening gap between the increasingly extreme political activists and those who believed that there was another way forward.

'I joined the local branch of the then Ulster Conservative and Unionist Party just at the time when the troubles really took hold. I felt that those who had been elected were not actually presenting our case properly on a number of issues. I would wish to stress that, while I wanted to represent the majority Protestant/Unionist viewpoint as a Christian minister, I was strongly against negative anti-Catholic propaganda. I believed that my place at that time was in the pulpit as a pastor to my congregation which was prospering spiritually, although some members were unhappy with my involvement in politics.

'Some politicians today are unhappy when the church gets involved in politics but I believe that as an institution in the community there are times when it cannot avoid doing so. The word "politics" comes from the Greek word "polis", meaning "the city". The church is always where the people are and is surely aiming for a time when there will be "a new city", the New Jerusalem, in God's kingdom. It must, therefore, make its voice heard by the decision makers in our land whose judgments affect all our lives. Above all, it is in the place of prayer for the country and the world that it can play a key role.'

In 1972, Martin was elected to office in the Ulster Unionist Council and progressed from there to become secretary and eventually vice-president. In 1975, tired of ministers pontificating from afar, he went into the Constitutional Convention by leave of Presbytery. He continued to preach regularly, supported in the ministry by his assistant, while a part-time deaconess helped with the time consuming task of pastoral visitation.

'Ministers may preach about moral standards and the like but when it comes to political issues, there was the risk of being at best misunderstood or, worse still, being ignored completely. I saw this as an opportunity to take part in a constitutional convention in which one would be in a better position to put forward views to the government. More importantly, I was invited to represent South Belfast at a time when things were in chaos.

'The Convention reported to the government, putting

up a paper for discussion but the talks failed when the minority groups insisted in having a place in executive government. The Unionists opposed this, stating that, in a democracy, only the electorate should have the power to hire and fire their rulers.'

While maintaining his interest in politics after the collapse of the Convention, Martin continued with his church activities, preaching and lecturing throughout Northern Ireland. Then, in 1981, his close friend and colleague, Robert Bradford, MP for South Belfast, was assassinated by the IRA at his advice centre.

'Murders are a regular occurrence in our land but when it comes to someone you know personally the horror of it can be overwhelming. I was stunned and saddened by his murder and had the difficult task of helping to find a replacement for his seat. One day, when I was conducting a funeral, a colleague said to me, "Don't you think you should be taking Robert's place, Martin?" I was taken aback as the thought had not entered my head to go into politics at this level.

'Humanly speaking it was not an attractive proposition. The same risks would confront me as had faced Robert but I began to pray specifically about it. In the course of my ordinary devotions I was challenged through reading Jeremiah to push a few doors and seek God's guidance. I decided to put myself forward for selection and was chosen. It was not an easy time for my family. My wife knew the dangers but was supportive as long as I felt that it was the correct thing to do. My eldest daughter was already married and the younger was still at home.'

As a family they had known the support and guidance

of God in their lives on many occasions. They had shared challenges and joys together. There had been sad times when they needed assurance above all things. Like the tragedy in 1974 when their youngest daughter Margaret, born to them shortly after they were bombed in Belfast, was killed in a car accident when out shopping with her mother. With God's help and the fellowship and support of friends they were wonderfully upheld during their bereavement.

'There were those among my friends and colleagues who told me that I was wrong to take such a step at this point in my life, some questioning whether I would be able to serve God better as a politician than as a minister of the gospel. Notwithstanding these turmoils, I went into the election in 1982 feeling sure that it was the right thing to do but with my mind heavy with the burden of my dying father. He passed away and was buried two days before voting took place. I look back now and recall the amazing inner peace that God gave me.'

Martin knew very well that he would not be able to sustain his parish ministry for long if he were elected and this was a part of his life that he knew he would miss. When elected he remained a minister of the church but without a charge to sustain. Certainly, he would continue to have regular invitations to preach at home and abroad but he enjoyed meeting and being among people to advise and help them spiritually. Interestingly, he has found that his life and work as an MP provide as many opportunities to help others as when he was the full time pastor of a congregation.

'I consider that what I now have is, in effect, an

extended parish. I find that people come to me as their MP during consultation times with problems which are ostensibly social, economic or political. But when we talk together it sometimes leads to a discussion on spiritual matters, more often than not at their initiative. Perhaps it is the "Rev" in front of my name, more than "MP" at the end, which catches their eye, but many doors have opened unexpectedly for Christian witness.

'This has happened even at an international level. I was part of a British delegation visiting an African country when we were being entertained by our hosts. The gathering was multi-national and multi-faith and I was seated beside a devout Muslim politician at the welcome dinner. I was taken aback when, during the meal, the gentleman asked, "What do you think about those people who say that Jesus was God and that he rose again after he was crucified?" I responded with, "Well, I have to say that I agree with them!" That led to an extended discussion and an opportunity to share my faith with him.

'It also made me very aware, as a politician and a Christian, that so often we bend over backwards to avoid saying anything which will cause offence but, in doing so, we may be missing an opportunity to share what we believe. While I do not believe in ramming my political or theological views down other people's throats, I do hold to the view that I should be ready to take the opportunity to share my opinions in a courteous manner when appropriate. "A word in season," the Bible says.'

His desire to continue to reach out to others has extended beyond normal boundaries. When he was elected to Westminster he learned that there was an all party group whose aim was to support Soviet Jews who were being persecuted in the USSR. He was included in one of the first cross party delegations of MPs who went to Moscow in 1983 to press for the release of the many soviet 'refuseniks' who had been imprisoned for their political and religious beliefs.

'We were able to meet, not only the well known, but also some not so well known dissenters, including scientists and religious leaders. I took some literature for them, including writings in Hebrew and translations of the Bible. That was a very interesting time and, in common with my fellow MPs, I am thankful for the freedom which prevails in our land to live and believe as we please, albeit with laws and other constraints which some challenge. But we must never take for granted our liberty to challenge what we believe to be unjust.'

His interest in the USSR saw his appointment as Vice Chairman of the All Party Committee on Soviet Jewry in 1983. In parliament he has held various posts including Party Spokesman on Foreign Affairs, and on Health and Social Security. He is a member of the Health Select Committee: he holds office in a number of all Party Select Committees and is a member of the United Kingdom Executive of the Commonwealth Parliamentary Association.

During his period as MP he has taken time to write on both political and Christian themes. He is a regular contributor to various church titles and is the author of a number of short publications. These include one on marriage guidance, *Till Death Us Do Part* and another entitled *Why a Presbyterian?*. More poignant is his booklet *Faith Under Trial* which he wrote following the untimely death of his young daughter.

Among his various political interests is the idea of federalism in Britain. The discussion paper, *A Federated People* outlines his belief that the United Kingdom would function better politically and economically if power were devolved from the centre.

Striking the balance between political and Christian standpoints is just as challenging for Martin Smyth as it is for other MPs.

'My theological training and background as a pastor do not make it less difficult when decisions have to be made and votes cast. Guidance from Scripture on how to deal with the grey areas comes no easier to me than to other Christian MPs. For some people "conscience" may simply end up meaning: "I've lost that vote and I'm going to go against you." But I believe that it should come from and be based on the Bible. However, there are many questions in life, many political decisions to be taken which do not have a specifically Christian answer. Try as I might, I cannot see a Christian perspective on Maastricht, for example. Some argue that the treaty has theological implications, that there is an attempt to "re-Romanise" Europe. Others argue that we should vote for it on the basis that it will open up a wider parish for the gospel!

'Among matters of conscience for me have been the issues of Sunday trading and abortion. I am on record as saying in the House of Commons, "How can we expect our nation to obey the laws of the land if we in this house do not take heed of the laws of God?" Having said that, I sought the support of those who do not hold to Christian beliefs as

I saw that both of these debates were as much about human rights and freedoms as about taking a religious stance. The Bible is strong on human rights. Also, many of the laws and much of the guidance are based on common sense, social and medical wisdom which we can now understand with our knowledge of things today.

'To further underline the dilemma at times, I know it would be foolish to suggest that all these issues are clear cut. Take abortion: some I know are totally against it at any cost. I go a long way down the line but I must admit to being challenged by the question of choice between the life of the mother or that of the unborn child. If the decision is to lose the life of the mother, a husband is bereft of a partner and other children may be motherless. That is not a solution I would support.

'The problem of a pregnancy resulting from rape is also debated. I would never ever condemn a girl or her parents if they decide to proceed with an abortion, for they need my prayers and support. But I would also point out that there are still opportunities for adoption today. God may make good out of the evil which has been perpetrated or the "mistake" which has taken place, if it is simply an unwanted pregnancy. After all, even in the recorded genealogy of Christ in the New Testament, there are children born out of wedlock and in dubious circumstances.

'The debate on capital punishment is one where there is cross party division and disagreement among Christian MPs. I do not believe that everyone who is charged with murder should be executed nor do I hold to the viewpoint that if God forgives the criminal we should not be prepared to take their life in certain circumstances. I believe that capital punishment is scriptural and that for certain acts of murder it should be carried out. The debate is complex, I accept, and it is not helped by reports of miscarriages of justice. I am also conscious that my own feelings have been coloured by the terrorism in Ireland. However, given the opportunity to discuss it again at Westminster I believe I would vote for restoration as a deterrent and a just retribution.

'We should not underestimate the influence which back-bench MPs can have on government policy. On a number of occasions I have seen bills returned to the floor of the Commons with up to one hundred amendments as a result of the probing and questioning of members on both sides of the House. Just as long sermons from the pulpit are not necessary to get the message across effectively, for an MP it may not be the lengthy oration or the loud voice of complaint which has the greatest effect but the quiet word at the right time in the House or to a minister.'

The intense security which Martin has to be under most of the time takes its toll. All around there are reminders of the horrors of terrorism and there are regular threats on the lives of public figures on the mainland as well as in Northern Ireland. He is now resigned to living under this shadow.

He recalls an early surgery where he went to meet constituents. There was quite a large presence of heavily armed police: remember, his predecessor, Robert Bradford, had been murdered at one such centre. While he was reassured by the security, he was not very happy about the

welcome which greeted callers at the surgery door. 'Have
you a problem to put to your MP?' sounded more like an
army orderly officer addressing a question to his troops,
while the orderly sergeant stands behind him, watching
carefully to see if anyone dared to raise a voice of complaint!

'While I don't believe I will ever really get used to it,
I have had to accept living in this way. All MPs, indeed
all those in public life, have to pay this price but there is
a sharp edge for those who live in, or are associated with,
Northern Ireland. The tension would be too great, the
burden unbearable, I am sure, if I did not hold to that sense
of calling which I have in the job I am doing.

'Of course I am afraid at times. Anyone who has no
sense of fear has no sense of feeling. I know I must seek
help from the security forces, I know I must be wise in all
that I do and say; but why should I go through life
worried, constantly looking over my shoulder? That is
what the terrorist hopes to achieve. I have to believe that
my life will end when God sees fit to take me to be with
Himself.'

There are those who question whether a Christian
minister should be involved in politics at all. One quote
to Martin after his election was, *Ye cannot serve God and
mammon*. He would have been delighted to reply to the
letter but, as is often the case, the writer had not appended
a name and address. As Martin pointed out, this text
refers, not only to Christian ministers and workers, but to
all followers of Christ.

'Perhaps one of the greatest weaknesses in the Church
is that too many who name the name of Christ, while they

would not soil their hands in the mud of politics, tend to keep close to mammon in business, pleasure or in other spheres. All must give Jesus Christ full allegiance as Lord and Master.

'As long as I am elected to this seat, and for as long as God wishes me to be here, I shall pray for a sense of purpose and continue to ask for His peace and guidance in my life.'

It is not easy to have a sense of peace in many parts of Northern Ireland. Peace movements have come and gone but the fear, the intimidation, the terror and the murders continue. Martin Smyth would be the last person to suggest that he alone could make such an impact on the political situation that there will be an early solution to the troubles in his country: rather he would stress that he is only one voice among many.

As he described it, 'I am doing the same sort of job as I did as a minister, it is just that I have a wider parish, a much larger congregation and there are others with me in the pulpit.'

5
THE RT. HON ALAN BEITH
Liberal Democrat MP for Berwick-on-Tweed

Aspirations and Inspirations

The worshippers in the little Methodist chapel remained attentive throughout the sermon and the young lay preacher felt sure that it had met with their approval. He had spent a long time preparing the talk to the rural congregation and, when he sat down after his well planned conclusion, he anticipated that the minister would announce the final hymn. Instead, after a brief word of thanks, the more experienced clergyman proceeded to flesh out his message, clearly implying that it had been too short for his liking.

This rather humbling experience at the start of Alan Beith's ministry on the rural circuit of churches did not discourage him. Undeterred, he continued with his theological studies and went on to become a well known Methodist lay preacher in the area. In any case, the remarks by the minister that day would be nothing compared to the heckling and barracking he would have to endure years later when he was elected to the House of Commons.

Despite his busy life now as Liberal Democrat MP for Berwick-on-Tweed, he still finds time to preach. As a gifted orator at Westminster during the week, the oppor-

tunity to prepare a sermon at weekends may be viewed by
some as simply an extension of his wish to share his
political views with another, more captive, audience away
from London.

While the content of an occasional sermon may reflect
his Liberal background, his desire to preach goes above
and beyond party politics. It springs rather from his
personal faith and commitment to Christ and a love for
the Word of God which he wishes to share with others. It
all started in his youth even before he became involved
with the Liberals.

He now lives with his wife and family in the North
East of England. But his roots are in fact in Cheshire
where he was born in Poynton, a mining village in attractive countryside. His father, a packer in a Manchester
factory, moved there when the business was transferred
to Cheshire after the terrible bombing of the city during
the last world war. The war ended when he was just two
years old and he recalls having a happy childhood. He
attended the local primary school from where he won a
scholarship to King's Grammar School in Macclesfield.
Six years later, to the delight of his parents, he gained
entry to Balliol College, Oxford, reading Philosophy,
Politics and Economics. Then it was on to do postgraduate research in Politics and Public Administration.

He certainly did not drift into politics, for it was very
much in his mind even when he was still at secondary
school. At the age of fourteen, he was keen to find out
more about the Liberal Party, so set out to find the name
of a local contact. He told me the story.

'It was the late 1950s and the Liberals had just won

their first by-election since the war from the Conservatives, at Torrington. I was interested in joining the Liberals so I looked up a directory and found that my Sunday
School superintendent at the local Methodist chapel was
the secretary. His response was, "Oh, nobody's asked to
join for a long time. I'll have to find a form for it."

'It was not simply their well publicised victory at
Torrington that persuaded me to find out more about the
party; nor was I following the example of my parents for
they were at that time working class Conservatives. Perhaps the main influences were at school, particularly by
some teachers, but it was also my reading of British
history and the early work of the Liberal Party when it
was in a position of great influence.

'At that time also, the Tory government were, in my
opinion, behaving fairly badly in relation to the desire for
independence of the African colonies. That fired many
young people of my age to embrace certain Liberal ideals.
Neither did the Labour Party appeal to me as it appeared
in those days to downgrade the rights of the individual.
Their views on collectivism and their promotion of the
necessity of belonging to the right union to be told what
to do, did not impress me at all as a teenager.'

In *Faith in Politics*, which he wrote in co-operation
with Conservative MP John Selwyn Gummer and Labour MP Eric Heffer, he explained why he was attracted
to the Liberal Party in particular:

'The application of Christian principles led me to choose
Liberalism and ... while I have no hesitation in com-
mending it to other Christians enthusiastically, in doing
so I cast no doubt on the commitment of those who draw

different political conclusions from the same basic
beliefs.'[1]

'From then on I began to assist in local electioneering
and in any way I could to support the Liberal cause in the
area. Later in my academic career I had it in mind to study
journalism when I left university with a view to becoming
a political correspondent. But I had the opportunity to go
to Nuffield College which gave me a taste of academic
life and some time later I was offered a post as lecturer in
politics at Newcastle University. This was one reason
why I moved North in 1966 and eventually became
actively involved in local politics in that part of the
country.'

During these formative teenage years in Alan's life,
the Methodists were also an early spiritual influence on
him. In his childhood days his parents were not frequent
church attenders (although they later became active members) but they did send him to the chapel Sunday School
where, after a period of rebellion against having to turn up
every Sunday, he became a more committed member.
Later he joined the church and taught in the Sunday
School. At grammar school, religious meetings and
discussion groups were organised and he began to attend
along with friends who were committed Christians.

'Arthur Noon, our minister, was an elderly man and
rather quaintly old fashioned in his style; but in a fascinating way he was greatly admired and respected by people
of all ages in the congregation. Perhaps reflecting his
mining background, he was very much a man of the
people. He was a superb preacher of tremendous depth

and range, belying the fact that he was entirely self-educated. I was greatly influenced by his ministry and, along with a growing number of my friends, became more interested and involved in Christian things. There followed a greater assurance that this was the correct path for me to take in my life.'

Arthur Noon also persuaded him to train as a lay preacher which he embarked upon during his time at university and completed following his graduation. His Christian interests extended to life at university when he preached from time to time as a member of the Methodist Society.

'It also gave me the opportunity to get out into the real world from a rather cossetted life at university. In many respects it heightened my Christian concerns as my understanding of people and society was broadened by the whole experience. In addition, I became involved with a magazine which provided a forum for discussion of Christian views. Latterly, I became news editor which exposed me to a very wide range of opinions, some of which I strongly disagreed with. I came across extreme modernism which bent over backwards to be all things to all men but ended up meaning very little to very few. I was the one being seen to promote the orthodox viewpoint in order to restore the balance. All in all it turned out to be an excellent educational opportunity for me.'

There may have been debates and some division over forms of church government in the Methodist church but, as Alan pointed out, there has never been a clear split in the denomination between evangelicals and non-evangelicals.

'The foundation of common principles comes traditionally from the days of Wesley and his firm conviction that God calls everyone. Preaching in towns, villages and on crowded hillsides, the reformer invited educated and uneducated, rich and poor, to hear and accept the good news, proclaiming that the gospel is for every man and woman and that all who believe can be saved.'

There is a substantial history of Methodist association with Liberalism in some parts of the country and with the Labour party in others; and there have always been some Conservative Methodists. As Alan explained in *Faith in Politics*, there was one event of note in the early 1900s.

'In 1905 there was an occasion when The Biblical Christians, a West Country Methodist sect of great local influence, which later became part of the modern Methodist Church, passed a resolution calling on the nation to "shake itself free from the incubus of a government dominated by the priest and the publican." It was, of course, a Tory government: the implication that West Country Bible Christians should vote Liberal hardly needed any further stress; and, so far as we know, they did.'[2]

Alan's balancing act as editor of that university magazine, his desire to bridge the gap between two theological extremes, was in many ways a mirror of his political viewpoint. It could be said that the Liberal Democrats have always sought to find the middle way in politics, a balance between two extremes. But, he would argue, certainly not in an attempt to be all things to all men so that nothing is ultimately achieved as real issues become blurred in the clamour for compromise.

As a trainee lay preacher he began to preach in local

churches and others in the Methodist circuit. At first there was a form of apprenticeship which involved going round with an established local preacher to help conduct services before going 'on trial', taking courses and examinations and then being assessed by others who would make reports after he had conducted a service.

'It was really quite a rigorous course, although I was given exemptions from some exams because of my university courses. The first sermons had to be preached in out of the way country chapels before I was allowed to take services in larger towns. In one of these rural villages I recall being surprised when the hymn singing was led, not by an organist, but by an accordionist.'

In September 1965, he was invited to attend a church meeting one evening to learn that he had passed all aspects of the training and was now 'licensed' as a Methodist local preacher. It was a momentous occasion, but that evening he had other things on his mind because the following day he planned to marry his fiancée Barbara, a science teacher whom he had met on the daily train journey to school.

During his time at Oxford he was more involved in studying and preaching than in politics, although he did stand on one occasion for a ward in a local election. But this changed somewhat after graduation. He took an active part in academic life at Newcastle but his interest in politics grew again and he was elected as a councillor in the Northumberland village in which he lived.

When there was the likelihood of a parliamentary election, he was encouraged to put his name forward to be the candidate, not only in his home constituency, but also at Berwick-on-Tweed, which the party had a better chance of winning.

'Although it is hard for members of other parties to appreciate, winning in those days was seen very much as a bonus to Liberals, who believe that campaigning for ideas and ideals is just as important as wresting a seat from an opponent. Nevertheless, the more promising seat was attractive so I stood there in 1970 and came third on an increased vote. In 1973, the year the Conservative government declared a state of emergency, just prior to the now famous three day week, there was a by-election in the constituency. I gained the seat, by a narrow margin of only 57 votes, after several recounts. There were three elections within a year and by the third my majority was still only 73!

'I can still recall the great sense of elation and relief, when I was elected on that first occasion, albeit by such a slender majority. To have to go through the process several times in close succession was nerve-wracking to say the least and I was entirely preoccupied by the whole experience. I was fortunate to have been given five years unpaid leave of absence by the university, which protected me from the possible threat of financial difficulty if I failed to hold the seat.

'To a great extent this was an answer to prayer as far as I was concerned as it enabled me to follow my chosen path with less anxiety than I might otherwise have had. I always believed that God was calling me to engage in service through politics. To become an MP would be an added bonus, I considered, but this was in the hands of the electorate!'

Alan Beith believes that his life and work as an MP are
natural extensions of his Christian service, a theme which
he expands on, again in *Faith in Politics*.

> 'The fundamental biblical source for Christian involve-
> ment in politics, I believe, lies in the teaching of Jesus
> about the responsibility to others. "When saw we thee
> an hungered, or athirst, or a stranger, or naked, or sick, or
> in prison and did not minister unto thee?... Inasmuch as
> ye did it not to one of the least of these, ye did it not unto
> me."
>
> 'The ministry of Jesus speaks by precept and exam-
> ple of the obligation to serve the needs of others.
> Experience teaches us that, although individual service
> remains central to Christian living, there are means now
> available to us of meeting need which require collective
> effort. We have discovered that with the resources on
> the scale available to the state it is possible to cure and
> treat illness to an extent not possible by individual or
> voluntary collective effort.
>
> 'Questions remain about what should be the balance
> of public and private, of collective and individual, in
> meeting those needs, but the perception that they exist
> and that the state has some part to play in meeting them
> is fundamental to Christian involvement in politics.'[3]

Since taking his seat at Westminster, Alan has had
many opportunities to serve in the wider sphere of politics. Among other things, he has been a representative to
the Council of Europe; chairman of the Sub Committee
on Architectural and Artistic Heritage of Europe; and a
member of the Western Union Assembly. In his party he
has served as Chief Whip; Spokesman on Foreign Af-

fairs; Treasury Spokesman; and was Depute Leader of
the Liberal Party from 1985-88. He is now Depute Leader
of the Liberal Democrats.

Elections come and go as do political aspirations and
opportunities. In a changing world it is frequently the
constants in life which sustain us. During election campaigns and while an MP he continued to engage in lay
preaching and valued the opportunity to get out and about
speaking to congregations in the North and North East of
England.

His Christian faith and church activities remain central supports in his life as much as a politician as a lay
preacher. He has never felt it necessary to give up this
ministry, although he has sought at times to spread out
commitments to allow time to be with his family. Among
other pastimes he enjoys walking, boating and listening
to and taking part in music.

In common with many other MPs I have spoken to,
Alan particularly values the support and encouragement
from his wife and family at home. With this background
he holds firmly to the belief that family life and values
should be promoted in society today.

'I cannot see how society can operate if it doesn't
sustain family life. Take this away and the main opportunity to learn to relate to others is removed. By this I
mean during difficult as well as happy times, for it is often
through trials and challenges that relationships are strengthened. I read the other day an apt quotation by Norman
Dennis who, when I knew him, was a Labour councillor
who opposed the intensive demolition of housing areas
and communities by the Sunderland Labour Council:

"Unless a child is brought up in the constant atmosphere of human beings, negotiating the business of getting on with one another, controlling their anger, knowing reconciliation, he or she cannot learn to be a member of an effective social group."

'Family life and Christian marriage are under threat and more and more children are being reared by single parents. As someone who is strongly opposed to abortion, I am bound to maintain that society should therefore be less censorious of single mothers who choose to bring up their children and deserve care, love and support. Yet there are so many problems facing one-parent families that we cannot possibly advocate this model as an alternative lifestyle.

'This dilemma may be answered by looking to the example of Jesus who condemned what was wrong quite vigorously while never diminishing his expression of love for the individual. The Bible has many examples of people who made mistakes in the past but who were forgiven. The woman whom Jesus met at the well had five husbands. He challenged her to change her ways but showed her compassion.

'What is the role of the Christian in politics today when faced with this situation? I do not think we have fully resolved that yet because society has a parallel dilemma in realising how it can express preference for certain values while not being unfair or damaging towards those who are the victims of failure to uphold those values: more so when the innocent victims are children.

'It is obvious that there should be adequate benefits for single parents so that children don't suffer. It is then

perceived by some that the best way to get support,
particularly with housing, is to have an illegitimate child.
Achieving the balance at a time of scarce resources is
very difficult indeed. My instinct as a Liberal, reflecting
the principle of the philosopher John Stuart Mill, is to try
to interfere as little as possible with the right of individuals to choose unless their decisions impinge on other
people's freedom. In *Faith in Politics*, I wrote:

> 'It is a principle of Liberalism that the state is there to
> help the individual lead his own life and to maximise
> his freedom to choose that life for himself. Collective
> solutions may be the only means of tackling some
> human problems, but their use must be recognized as
> posing potential threat to individual freedom: we should
> constantly be striving to protect the individual from the
> dominance of the state.'[4]

'However, Members of Parliament must also be aware
that changes in the law to permit greater freedom can in
effect give a signal that what was previously regarded as
"wrong" is now acceptable, if not totally "right". What is
legal may not be morally correct. When changing laws on
issues like abortion and divorce we always run the risk
that we make ethical what was once regarded as unethi-
cal. The same could be said for something like Sunday
trading when what we are allowed to do can subtly
change the climate of opinion, which in turn may lead to
a further erosion of standards. Politicians may prefer to
do things which are popular but when they analyse the
situation they realise that it can be more complex than
they first thought.'

We spoke about the responsibility which man must take for the environment, an issue which he also raised in *Faith in Politics*.

'The Christian holds that we are stewards of this earth, which we have on trust from God. It follows that we must care for it, not merely for the present, but also for the future. That is a long-standing emphasis of Liberal thinking. We believe that all policies should be examined from an environmental and ecological standpoint, and we have been critical of those aspects of industrial, energy and agricultural policy which have lacked that perspective.' [5]

'Other areas of challenge for the Christian include defence, crime and punishment. I have friends who are pacifists but I do not hold to that belief. I accept that there has to be a physical force available on the side of law and order but as to the basic question, "Is there such a thing as a just war?" theologians have debated it down through the centuries and I would not presume to offer a simple definitive answer in the space of an interview.

'There is a related aspect of Christ's example: his indignant refusal to accept that evil should go unchallenged. He turned over the table of the Temple moneylenders because their shady dealings despoiled the courts of God. He railed against the hypocrisy of the scribes and the Pharisees. ... Anger at evil is a proper Christian sentiment and has driven Christians into political action through many centuries.

'It was anger which drove Wilberforce on through the decades until the slave trade was abolished. It was a refusal to accept the continuance of a great evil that

made Christian politicians fight for laws to bring children out of the mines.' [6]

'Some might say that we need to return to basic
biblical principles to find answers. It would be fine if it
were easy to do so but the Bible does not necessarily give
answers to the more complex dilemmas. In fact, the Bible
may challenge us by asking questions without proposing
simple answers. When questioned by the religious leaders of his day, Jesus sometimes replied by posing another
question, not giving an answer.'

The Liberal Democrats have not been in a strong
position of power at Westminster for many years but
there have been times when their number has influenced
the outcome of a vote. There is the apparent luxury of
being able to promote an ideal which they know can never
be implemented but which may win them popular appeal.
Notwithstanding the persuasive arguments which they
may put forward in a debate on the floor of the House, I
asked Alan whether this was a problem for him as a
Christian MP at Westminster.

'I always hope that I will uphold integrity and honesty
in debate or when I cast my vote. How tempting it would
be to advocate, for example, the doubling of all state
benefits to appeal to the electorate! It may seem like a real
vote winner, but where would the money come from? On
the contrary, our party has never shied away from making
proposals which are not overt vote winners. For instance,
it was our policy at the last election to state openly that we
might need to increase taxes to improve our education
system.

'I know that there are many MPs who hold to the same Christian beliefs as I do but who would be totally opposed to my party's point of view. That does not absolve them or me from being correct in our political dealings with each other nor when faced with the demand for an honest answer to questions in the House. There is the temptation for MPs to trade propaganda or to knowingly fasten on to one minor point which is "sellable". I hear too often evasive and blatantly dishonest replies which disturb me greatly and which serve to undermine the democratic principles of parliament.

'Particularly now that debates are broadcast and widely reported in the media, it may bolster the idea that all politicians are charlatans, people not to be trusted with your loose change far less the family silver.'

Those who are acquainted with Alan Beith and work alongside him at Westminster or in Church activities, know that these are not empty words. Whether preaching from the pulpit, arguing his case in parliament or taking part in television debates he is widely respected for the open and honest stand that he takes on all topical issues. His political stance is radically Liberal but he is not slow to make his voice heard in the country on matters relating to Christian standards and beliefs.

1. *Faith in Politics* by John Selwyn Gummer, Eric Heffer and Alan Beith (First published in Great Britain in 1987 by SPCK, Holy Trinity Church, Marleybone Road, London, NW1 4DU. 2. ibid. 3. ibid. 4. ibid. 5. ibid. 6. ibid.

6
ALISTAIR BURT
Conservative MP for Bury

Principles and Politics

Before he entered the chamber of the House of Commons that evening he had made up his mind to resign from his position as a Parliamentary Private Secretary. He knew that there would be repercussions within the Conservative Party and it was likely that his own career would be affected. As a young MP, elected at the age of 28, he had quickly made his mark bringing in fresh ideas and had impressed the minister as one who would respond readily to the challenge of additional responsibility. In short, Alistair Burt had a bright future ahead of him, elections and party politics permitting.

The same basic principles which had persuaded him to enter politics as a Conservative MP in the first place were now causing him to question the decision his party was asking him to take. When the division bell sounded, he abstained in protest against the Bill being tabled that day, despite the application of a three line whip by the Government.

When the Sunday Trading Bill was first discussed several years ago he was deeply disturbed by the proposals and made his feelings clear to the Government at every opportunity. He was not alone on his side of the

House as others had voiced their opinions on a number of occasions. As far as he was concerned, the issue was more than a reflection of his left of centre political leanings inside the Conservative Party; it was a matter of conscience and belief.

The Bill, to allow normal trading on Sundays in England and Wales, was being opposed by MPs for a number of reasons. For some it was objection to possible exploitation of employees; for others it sprang from a belief in the right of shopworkers to have time for relaxation and recreation at the weekend. Alistair supported both these arguments but also promoted the Christian dimension, the biblical principles which are reflected in these social and human rights.

Since his childhood, Sunday had been a special day. He learned that it should be a time to relax, be with the family, meet friends and a day when he attended the local parish church in Bury with his parents. His father was the local GP and Alistair recalls his example of Christian living in and out of his practice. His heavy working hours meant much extra work for Alistair's mother, and her example of motherhood, together with his father's quiet but sure faith made a great impression on him and his elder brother David.

At Bury Grammar School, where he was a pupil for thirteen years from the age of five, there were regular morning prayers, readings and hymns at assembly. Unaware of it at the time, life at school and the guidance of certain teachers had a great influence on him spiritually.

'I believe that we often underestimate the influence that teachers can have on their pupils,' said Alistair. 'I recall many teachers whose lives and attitudes had a positive effect on me. In particular, I remember John Bisson, my R.E. teacher. A Methodist, he ran the school Christian Fellowship and provided a base for many of the beliefs I have today. He was later joined by Peter Hampson, who introduced me to a different style of worship through more modern music, which brought life into my Christian faith as a young man.

'The life and witness of my parents, first of all and later of many of my teachers, brought home to me that Christian service was more to do with how people lived from Monday to Saturday than it was about how they behaved on a Sunday: but, that time of rest, reflection and replenishment on the Lord's Day is a central and important point in the week; a day worth safeguarding for the nation.

'Reg Smith, the rector of my local church, has been and remains a great support to me also. His teaching, his pastoral care and advice as I grew in the faith, prepared for confirmation and moved towards a career, were pivotal in shaping my life.'

On reading these comments today some of his teachers might be forgiven for saying, 'And he certainly needed it!' for he was known to be a bit of a rascal, the class comedian during his early days at school. He is now aware that there was considerable concern among the staff that his behaviour would hinder his academic progress, particularly as he approached transition to the secondary course.

One teacher, Tom Spencer, frustrated to see him failing to reach his full potential, took him aside after class one day and said, 'If gold were to rust, what would iron do?'

'I was taken aback by his strange remark,' Alistair recalled, 'but it became clear that people felt that I could achieve more than I had done to date if I set my mind to it. In his own way, my teacher was suggesting that I was undervaluing myself and possibly ruining my future if I did not reach my academic potential. He was also unhappy that I was not an influence for good among my peers, preferring instead to relax and have fun when work should have been the order of the day.

'That might have washed over me had it not suddenly occurred to me that I had disappointed people whom I genuinely respected at home and in school. That was a turning point. I was assisted further by Albert Shaw, a retired teacher, who put in extra work to ensure that my grades improved dramatically. He believed in my abilities, and I began to take things more seriously.'

Coincidentally, Alistair was challenged to take the faith of his childhood forward into greater commitment to Christ in his early adult life. It was not a dramatic conversion experience, more a conscious decision to choose a way of life which would be more fulfilling and meaningful than had previously seemed possible.

'The academic and spiritual side of my life began to move forward in tandem as a result of this change in nature and attitude which took place in my early teens. I realised that what God wanted me to do was not to reach for some unattainable goal but to make the most of the talents that He had given me, to be all that I could be for Him and for my fellow men and women. To do otherwise would not have been simply to neglect without consequence but to betray God and deny what He had planned for me.'

In his teens, personal prayer and Bible study became a supportive time for him rather than just a ritual to follow as directed. That said, however, he did not suddenly move from being class comedian to become the school's model of behaviour. He retained a keen sense of humour. He was the same Alistair Burt in other respects also but, given more responsibility as he progressed through school, he was appointed Head Boy before he left the hallowed portals. No sign of rust then!

He gained a place to read law at St John's College, Oxford and in 1976 became president of the university law society. He enjoyed college life very much and during his time there became involved in Christian activities when he was influenced by Bishop Graham Dow and Dr Anthony Phillips, whose ministry impressed him greatly. At Oxford he had the opportunity to meet Christians from many backgrounds and helped with evangelical outreach in and out of university.

After graduation in 1977 he articled in a solicitor's practice but he admits now that he did so more out of duty to the faculty he had chosen than out of a genuine desire to make a career in law. He had a half-hearted attitude to the professional exams he had to take and envied those graduates whose degree allowed them to choose from a variety of pathways. As a consequence, he failed. He did succeed at a later date but it was a salutary experience for someone who had passed every exam up to then.

'I would not wish to spiritualise this in any way,' he

elaborated, 'for I cannot say now that I felt that God was calling me elsewhere. I was at an intellectual crossroads in my life, not a spiritual one. I did not feel challenged by the career I had chosen. This is not to deny the direction which God may have planned for me, but my initial commitment had been to serve people in whatever sphere I was in. Law happened to be what I was doing, a decision I had taken at an early age, and perhaps that in itself was a problem for me. I did not really know what I was going in for: perhaps I had a romantic image from courtroom lawyers on television who won all their cases and fought off corruption at every turn!'

Politics seemed an attractive alternative, an opportunity to be of service at the sharp end, as it were. He had dabbled in politics while at school when he joined the Bury Young Conservatives. He became more active as time went on and began to get involved in local electioneering. He thoroughly enjoyed the cut and thrust of debate and the challenge of being a Conservative in a marginal northerly constituency. But why Conservative and not one of the other parties?

'I could trot out some ideological reason but that would be dishonest. At that point in time it was basically because I was brought up in a Conservative household. Although I later had some reservations about certain policies and sit more to the left of the party than my parents, I was more concerned about the economic direction of the Labour party and the influence of their extreme left wing. Later life confirmed me in my view that Conservative economics work better than Socialist economics.

'But social concerns remain as high on my agenda
now as they did when I tramped the streets of Bury seeing
poverty and deprivation in many of the less salubrious
areas within my father's practice. I hold firmly to the
belief that Conservative policies cannot ignore these
issues, and the people affected by them.'

He gave politics a miss while at Oxford. But when he
qualified and moved down to London he felt that there
was a gap in his life, which neither his position as a
lawyer, nor even his active participation in the local
church, adequately filled. Along with some friends he
was soon back into politics and in 1982 was elected to
Harringay Borough Council at the age of 26. He recalled
that period in his life.

'Again, I hesitate to spiritualise what was to a great
extent an intellectual leaning, but I certainly did make a
point of asking God what I should do with my life and
many of the friends around me were also committed
Christians who understood my position. I took the plunge
and contacted the local Conservative Association to offer
my services, having decided to enter public life in this
way. From that day to this I have had a sense of peace
about what I chose to do and have felt more fulfilled as a
result. The move seemed to be the final part of the jigsaw
in my life at that time.

'Many of my Christian friends are active in other
parties for similar reasons and I am very aware that, had
I been brought up somewhere else, in different circumstances, I could well be representing another political
viewpoint but with the common goal of service to the
community. To put it more humorously, being involved

in public life is my calling; being a Conservative into the bargain is my problem! God is not a paid up member of any party.'

Selected to stand for Bury North in 1983, he was elected to Parliament as one of the youngest MPs at that time. In fact, that year turned out to be a momentous one for him. In his Young Conservative days a young lady caught his eye. Eve Twite was also active in the party and was soon to become his running mate in more ways than one. They were engaged just after the council elections in 1982 and decided to marry in April the following year, unaware that the General Election would be called then.

'The election was called just after we returned from our honeymoon and we went straight to Bury after that; so politics have been part of our life together from day one. The hectic schedule of a politician is not conducive to married bliss but at least Eve had some idea of what she was letting herself in for before she said, "I do ...".'

Alistair spoke highly of the help his wife has been to him, how her increasing faith has sustained them both in times of difficulty. Being assured that this was what God wanted them to do has strengthened them in their calling and in their relationship. As well as taking part in local church activities Eve is involved with other MPs' wives in a supportive group known as the Wives Parliamentary Fellowship (see chapter 8). As Alistair put it, 'Only a member's wife can understand what a member's wife is going through, so it is an important fellowship to be involved in.

'The support of my wife is crucial in the work I do. Before we had a family she was my secretary and I know that at times she felt under enormous pressure. She is the homemaker for our two children, Hazel, who is 7 and Matthew, 6. The single worst thing about the whole escapade I embarked upon is the lack of opportunity to be at home as often as I would like. I do my best to minimise the effect that this has on my family.

'To a certain extent the children accept it, as they have known nothing else, but it can be very hard at times for Eve. Holidays are sacrosanct and we make the most of the opportunity to relax, have fun and renew our relationships because I miss them very much at other times. We thoroughly enjoy attending Spring Harvest most years and are spiritually and physically renewed by the experience.

'But I have to confess that political life is very wearing on the family, and I worry that to a certain extent the price of my very attractive career is being paid by them. They have given me a great deal, and I must make sure they are not asked to give too much.

'I gave up one life in going into politics to fulfil what I believed was right for me. It is not impossible that I may have to consider giving up another life for a while in order to fulfil my proper obligations to my family. I think I would still be true to what God wants me to be.'

He certainly has a busy life, now as Under Secretary of State at the Department of Social Security, a post which he has held since 1992. Prior to that he was appointed Parliamentary Private Secretary to the Rt Hon Kenneth Baker MP, when he was in various ministerial positions. But the stance that he felt he had to take on the Sunday Trading Bill could have stopped his promising career in its tracks.

'I knew that I could be laying my future on the line and I waited apprehensively for the result. To the surprise of many, the Government was defeated that night but the saving grace for me, and others who abstained with me, was that the Government had totally misjudged the mood of the backbenchers. In addition, they had been bold enough to apply the whip on what was widely held across the House to be as much a matter of conscience and belief as a party political proposal. We argued with the Home Secretary and warned him of the consequences of proceeding. They received a bloody nose when they failed to gauge the likely outcome before applying a three line whip. It was also seen by the opposition as a clear message to us not to take our large majority for granted and to appear to abuse our strong position.

'To be fair to the Government, they recognised that it had been a mistake. In turn, the Chief Whip refused to accept my resignation. I am not aware that my stance as a raw MP did me any harm and to the best of my knowledge it did not hinder my promotion prospects. In saying that, however, I do not wish to sound as if I was claiming the moral high ground or boasting about my spiritual triumph. Other colleagues played a more significant part in the action.'

In common with other MPs, the Parliamentary Christian Fellowship has been a great support to him during his time in the House. Having always looked for fellowship whenever he embarked on some new venture; at university or law school, for example, it was a natural thing for him to seek it when he became an MP. There was a special reason for Alistair, as he explained.

'Frank White, the man I defeated in 1983 to become MP, was the sitting Labour member for the area, although there were boundary changes before the election. I thought a very great deal of him, for he had been an excellent constituency MP. I learned that he was a member of the Parliamentary Christian Fellowship. After the election I went to see him and spoke about taking his place in the fellowship as I had found out that he would be greatly missed in the group, which goes above and beyond party politics.'

He is also encouraged by the opportunity to join a cross-party group of MPs invited to meet with the Speaker once a month to share communion in St Margaret's Westminster. A significant influence on his life in parliament is Anthony Cordle who has a Christian ministry among MPs and business people in London.

'When I was taking part in the election campaign, Anthony was in Bury and introduced himself to me, having noticed my church commitment on the literature. Unknown to me at the time, he had gone there to canvass for Frank during the election! When I took my seat at Westminster we renewed our acquaintance and he has been a friend ever since.'

When Anthony mentioned that there was a vacancy in a group going on a fact finding mission to South Africa and invited him to consider joining them, Alistair was initially sceptical.

'Deeply unsympathetic to the right wing regime, I made it clear that I did not wish to take part in anything that appeared to give comfort to politicians there who may be looking for international credibility. When he

assured me that it was to support people working in South
Africa for peace and reconciliation and that other Christians from different parties in the House would be going
along, I was keen to learn more.'

So often the outside world considers such visits by
MPs as nothing other than 'junketing' at the taxpayer's
expense. However, this was by no means an African
safari, as they soon found out. It was enjoyable and
interesting but a gruelling schedule had been arranged for
them. The visit with Simon Hughes, Liberal Democrat
and Peter Pike, Labour was to be an event which had a
great impact on him, and changed all their lives. They
have maintained their commitment to and contact with
the country and have made four visits in recent years to
renew past acquaintances and foster new relationships.
Accommodation has always been provided in people's
homes and meetings with those in high office have taken
place away from civil servants. Their aim throughout has
been to show solidarity and support at a personal level.

The 1986 visit coincided with the riots that destroyed
about twenty thousand homes in the Crossroads Squatter
Camp, outside Capetown. Alistair's enduring memory of
that trip is of the contrast between the horror of Crossroads, and attending a church service in the township of
Alexandria, near Johannesburg.

'In the midst of the devastation and terrible squalor,
with clouds of dust rising behind the car, we stopped at the
church. Inside we saw the Mothers Union dressed in
immaculate, white traditional costume. The enthusiasm
of their welcome showed tremendous optimism and energy even in the midst of the hardest conditions. Above

all, forgiveness–the outstretched black hand, putting aside generations of injustice. But then, we could never have envisaged what is happening now.'

One outcome of their contacts with the country has been regular prayer for South Africa. On most Wednesday evenings when the House is sitting they meet to share together and pray for that troubled part of the world. Their last visit was in November 1993 and they are committed to visit South Africa again whenever they are able to do so to offer whatever support appropriate at this time of change in the country.

Alistair sees opportunities to travel to consider concerns beyond the confines of parliament as 'added bonuses', time to share and have fellowship with other MPs. However, it is day-to-day issues which remain central to the work he does.

'The main challenge for me is to try to resolve dilemmas for which, to be completely honest, there might not be any clear spiritual guidance. I can openly say that I did not hear any clear voice from God about the poll tax or the abolition of the Greater London Council, to give examples. I believe that God sets up governments to do the best they can in an imperfect world and to work from Christian principles.

'Paul's comments in Romans about the authority of government is an oft quoted passage for Christians. I believe that government and authority is necessary in our secular world, for God likes order in His world and good government produces good order. I believe God also loves variety - that is why human beings have differing views as to how to deliver good government to each other.

But we live in a world where people's human nature can act for ill as well as good. It must be one of the purposes of government to ensure that the evil does not dominate the good, though of course this can be exceptionally difficult.

'The political philosophy I have chosen is one which recognises that the grain of God-given human nature for people is to seek to achieve, to look after those around one and also to look after one's neighbour. Individuality is to be highly prized but so also is a sense of community. I find a traditional Conservative philosophy enables me to put such feelings into practice in everyday politics but, as with all politicians, I recognise that my own party is not perfect and that occasionally I must differ from it and argue within it for change. If this were not to happen, then every political party's programme would be fixed and irremovable, and we would all be automatons! I do not believe such a charge can be levelled at most of our politicians.

'If Christians feel called to public service in politics but then shy away from it, fearing that they are treading into murky waters, they have to answer the question that if they do not do so, who takes their place? There will always be people seeking secular power, glory and wealth, who will be prepared to use politics as stepping stones. One hopes that the Christian in active politics works from a different reference point and seeks solely to do his or her best in this chosen field. I do not believe it makes me immune from errors of policy, nor does it guarantee electoral or political success. It should however give me a determination to attempt to find the right path and conduct my work in politics to the highest possible standards.

'Very few political issues have only one side. Most are multi-faceted and politicians will emphasise different things in their attempt to get to the root cause of the problem and set it right. For example, how does one make a judgment on levels of benefit? We would all seek to ensure that people have an adequate source of income but how do we ensure that they take the opportunity of work if it is offered? If benefit levels are too high and individuals choose not to work but to remain on benefit, is this a good or a bad thing?

'Again, in relation to housing and homelessness, it must be good to ensure that youngsters driven away from home have shelter and an income. But should provision go much further than that and if it does, does that provide any sort of perverse incentive for people to leave home and for families to become even more broken? These are difficult issues, capable of more than one answer, and probably capable of more than one answer which is right.'

I put it to Alistair that some people believe that the Conservative Government is less concerned about the problem of unemployment than members of the Opposition. Indeed, some maintain that high unemployment is part of a larger economic strategy supported by the party.

'I care as much as my friends and colleagues in other parties do but I hold to a different approach to solving it. I don't believe that such a large problem will be solved by subsidies only but rather by seeking an improvement in the way people conduct themselves in the market. To put it bluntly, that is what makes me a Conservative and not a

Socialist. But I like to think that whatever I do is with the same motive of love and concern for my neighbours and for the ultimate benefit of the whole community.

'There is a requirement to live up to the highest possible standards in decision making and in one's personal life; to ensure that any decisions will be taken for the greater good and not for selfish reasons. I do not find the process getting any easier for me as the years go by. Indeed, when in a position of power or authority it becomes more difficult as the personal repercussions are greater if a mistake is made. But my faith helps me as I have a commitment to serve other people to the best of my ability.

'In Social Security and Welfare, where I am at present, I have to take decisions which reflect the needs of the country as a whole and not only those that confront me when I meet individuals, even if I cannot but acknowledge the immediate straits they are in. It can be deeply agonising if I long to see benefits being raised to more tolerable standards when the country does not have the wherewithal to do so. As a Christian those things weigh heavily on me.

'Christian voices are raised in many ways in politics. The desire to serve, to be involved, to give of your best, to work with a team, is very strongly expressed in the process of government. There will be times when you don't always agree with your colleagues' decisions but, providing it is not a strong matter of conscience, you are willing to go with the team. The hope is that you will be able to improve upon it, as it may be possible to do on the inside. Change is possible behind the scenes and the role of the backbenchers is well known in this regard, as some governments have found to their cost.

'Christian voices of concern or even outrage can come also from outside politics, in the community and in the church. All these can influence politicians in parliament and ultimately the voters at the ballot box. A perennial source of entertainment in the press is the so-called "rift" between Church and State. Although my entire philosophy of life is orientated against feeling ill will towards people, I must say the way our press and media seek to sensationalise and trivialise matters of seriousness has distressed me over the years I have been in public life. Politicians are not innocents and they know that a cheap or ill-considered phrase will give them far more publicity than a thoughtful remark or speech. But for some time both written press and visual media have pandered to a drift in society towards an ever shorter concentration span. Accordingly, unless an idea is conveyed in a small number of words, or on a short piece on television, the general public will have been moved on to something else. It is a distressing trend and I cannot believe that the declining interest in the political process is not associated in some way with such trivialisation of issues.

'It must be right for the Church to speak out on public issues. As a Christian I welcome what the Church says on these day to day matters and rarely feel threatened by it. The Church must, however, be careful to guard against two things. Firstly, it must avoid entering the party political fray. If the Church is prepared to come down to my level and debate on my terms about party politics, then I

am going to win every time, and I am going to fight to win.
The Church has an infinitely more powerful message
than any political one I can proclaim and it does the Church
no good if it fights on my terms rather than its own.

'Secondly, there is the danger that the Church might
fail to promote its own message as effectively as it pro-
motes concerns in other fields. It can be of little surprise
that over the past twenty years or so the greatest growth
we have seen in the Anglican Church domestically has
been associated with the revival of the evangelicals and
Bible based worship and teaching.

'So the Church must keep its voice. But it must, in
speaking about social and political issues, remember
from where it derives its authority. It does not derive its
authority from any political ideology but from Jesus
Christ, His message and His suffering.

'The Government and the Church do not always have
the same job to do. Whoever is in government will find
difficulty in discharging all its tasks as fairly and equally
as the Church might wish and the Church will do well to
keep its role as adviser, friend and guide, as well as critic.
I find my local church in Bury does just that. I can expect
comment and criticism when things go wrong but immense personal support for the tasks I have to perform.
They also support my wife and family very strongly and
I believe this to be exactly the right balance. I have good
Christian friends who I do not expect to vote for me at the
end of the day but who I know, once I am there, give me
wholehearted personal support as well as praying from
time to time that the light will dawn on me in relation to
certain matters!

'This is the sort of relationship I would like to see nationally between Church and State. I believe it is actually a position much closer to reality than the press and television would have us believe. I enjoy the opportunity of sharing political and social comment with Church leaders, where I find we are more in agreement on most things than the public would necessarily expect. It is sad that conflict and confrontation receive so much publicity rather than our mutual respect.'

In closing, I asked Alistair to comment on how he felt when some Christians, genuinely concerned about the effect of government policies on the morale of the country, raised voices in opposition to them.

'Some voices I hear can be hurtful. For example, "How can you be a Christian and a Conservative?" some people may ask in reaction to a particular government policy. It is little reassurance at the time to know that on another occasion, with a different issue, a question in the same vein could be put to one of my Labour colleagues by a critic of that party's policies.

'What it boils down to is that my relationship with Christ and the fellowship I can have with His people, of whatever political shade or personal creed, is not dependent on my voting pattern within parliament. I would be sad if my friends, or indeed any of my constituents, believed otherwise.'

7

DONALD ANDERSON
Labour MP for Swansea East

Through Christian Spectacles

In the 1960s, anyone who knew of Donald Anderson's
Welsh working class background and socialist roots may
have suggested that he was a rather atypical member of
the Her Majesty's Diplomatic Service. Whether or not
this was the case, it was certainly unusual for someone,
whose theological inclination was decidedly nonconformist, to become an Anglican church warden in the
British Embassy in Hungary where he was posted.

Over a cup of coffee in the lounge of the attractive new
offices for members of parliament, situated opposite the
Palace of Westminster, Donald took time out of his busy
morning to tell how this interesting situation came about.
He spoke of a career which took him from Swansea, the
'ugly, lovely town' of Dylan Thomas, to university; then
to London and abroad, before eventually fulfilling his
dream to return to Wales and the politics of his forefathers.

Born and brought up in Swansea, in a caring home,
where his parents were irregular attenders at the local
Baptist chapel, he was taken to Sunday School from the
age of two by his elder sister. When he reached his teens
he was playing a full part in the youth activities of the
congregation.

'It was not a home where there was an abundance of books nor where Christian things were openly discussed,' he told me. 'Neither were there family prayers and other key signs of devotion, but it was a home where it was expected that the children would go along to the local chapel, normally three times on a Sunday. Those were days when all my friends on the street attended chapel regularly. It was as much a social as a religious event for us.

'I used to shine in the Sunday School Scripture examination. So the message of the Bible was well known to me and I was, from time to time, challenged by it; but it would be true to say that I was not always totally convinced that it was the life I should follow. There were occasions, in my middle and late teens, when I was attending Swansea Grammar School, when my commitment became stronger: and there were times at University College when I was filled with doubts and it became less so. Although there were periods of drift when I questioned the faith of my upbringing, I know that there was never a real severance from the Lord but it wasn't until I was in my early twenties, after I left university, that my commitment became overriding. There were a number of influences on me and I am aware of a few of them.

'One cannot but be affected by one's background, particularly where a Christian atmosphere exists, even if much of the Christian spirit was not fresh, but the afterglow of great revivals of the past. I look back now and recognise the influence of my Sunday School teacher and others in the chapel. Perhaps I wanted to ignore these when I went to university, widened my horizons and tried to find faith on my own. Then, when I went to London to join the Diplomatic Service, I recall the words of encouragement and the kindness shown to me by an elderly gentleman who stayed in the house where I was lodging, and who went with me to the local Baptist chapel. I remember listening to the long expositions of Dr Martyn Lloyd-Jones on Friday evenings at Westminster Chapel, along with many "hungry sheep" looking up and certainly being well fed!'

Donald's interest and involvement in politics began when he joined the Labour Party at the age of seventeen. At university he became chairman of the local Labour Club and, after graduating with a first in History and Politics, made the rather unusual jump from there to the senior branch of the Diplomatic Service. Opening with an amusing anecdote, he told me why he had joined the Labour movement and not one of the other parties.

'I recall the words of one of the great Labour pioneers, Bruce Glasier. He was brought up in the city of Glasgow and, when asked such a question, replied simply, "Glasgow". If I wanted to be short and to the point, I could reply in similar vein with "Swansea" for, in that city also, choosing to follow socialism was like a fish in water – as natural a thing for me to do as it was for my contemporaries. It was a community of poverty but, for many historical reasons, one where an egalitarian ethos prevailed. My grandfather, an old pioneer railway trade unionist, recounted how he had thrown a brick at "Winston Churchill's troops" during the Llanelli strike in 1911, and spoke about Bob Smillie, the Scottish miners' leader who, when told by the mine owners that their capital was sunk in the pit, replied that it was his men's lives that were sunk below ground.

'As a further example, I remember being very proud on learning that my mother, at school during the First World War, had maintained a close friendship with a classmate whose father was German even when the girl was ostracized by her fellow pupils.

'It is probable that the established church in Wales had traditionally been linked to the English, Conservative way of thinking, although it is much less so now. It was the nonconformists, grouped together because of language and commitment to industrial South Wales, who won the hearts of the majority of Welsh people. One cannot ignore the very strong links which existed between Welsh nonconformity and the Labour Party. In Wales there never was much of a working class Conservative vote, unlike Scotland which I am told did have at that time.

'Welsh people who became involved in the trade union movement, gained confidence, learned to speak in public and developed organisational skills through their life and work in the chapel. The deacons, who were the leaders of their own folk, would naturally become the leaders of their community. It is easy to romanticise, and I am sure that there are many examples to the contrary, but there certainly was a very close interweaving between the chapels and the working class movement, whether expressed through the trade unions or in the Labour Party.'

It was during his first term at university that Donald met Dorothy Trotman, a fellow undergraduate who later studied for a doctorate in biogeography. Dorothy, the

daughter of missionaries in Bolivia, had come at the age
of seven to board at Emmanuel Grammar School, part of
the Bible College of Wales, before going on to higher
education. Between arrival in Britain from Bolivia and
going up to university she met up with her parents on only
one furlough. If being separated from her family at a
tender age and having to make a life in another country
was a traumatic experience, when she met Donald
Anderson she soon found that an interesting future lay
ahead of her.

Donald joined the Diplomatic Service in London in
1960, while Dorothy continued with her thesis, before
they got married three years later, after he ended the break
in their relationship by revisiting her in the unromantic
setting of her laboratory. She submitted her completed
thesis on a Friday and they were married on the Saturday.
By the Monday evening of the same weekend they were
in Hungary, where Donald took up post as Third Secretary in Chancery.

'In the Diplomatic Service I worked alongside many
very fine people. There was a great family atmosphere in
the place, a real sense of community, albeit in an "officer
and gentleman" way. I was by status just that! Being
Welsh, nonconformist, and from a working class background, I was rather atypical in the service but I made
some very good friends, many of whom are now ambassadors and remain our friends.

'That was when we were asked to take on the job of
church wardens. None of the Anglicans in the service
wanted to do it so Dorothy and I volunteered. Not being
members of the established church, special permission

for us to take up the post had to be sought from the Bishop of Fulham in whose diocese Hungary came at that time. There was a place of worship at the embassy, an ordinary room which we re-arranged for the occasion, and the chaplain used to come once a month from the Anglican church in Vienna to take services. There was also the opportunity for a certain degree of outreach to the rather ageing British community, who were affectionately known as "The Ancient Britons", and in the wider community; where, incidentally, Dorothy and I became men's and women's diplomatic table tennis champions. One of my less glittering moments was when I mistakenly ushered the Bishop of Fulham into a broom cupboard and closed the door after him, when he requested a quiet room to robe!

'Only too aware that we were living "behind the Iron Curtain" it was very encouraging for us to have some contact with local Christians. We made a point of attending worship at a local Lutheran church at the Vienna Gate and we went down to a countryside place called Albertirsa. We still keep in touch with Christian families in Hungary, corresponding and visiting each other from time to time. Indeed, the son of one of the couples with whom we had fellowship in the 1960s, is now a member of the Hungarian parliament. I was very pleased when he telephoned me one Sunday in 1989 with the good news that he had just won a by-election. He was proud to emphasize that his victory marked the occasion of the first by-election which the Communist party had lost since 1947.

'We knew that people we met in the church were "safe" as they would not come to our home but only meet us in the park; anyone who came to our home must have had official permission and was, therefore, suspect. I've also had open house with a Sunday School for about twenty students from Ghana, with a number of whom we remain in contact today.

'Although left of centre in my political leanings, I fitted well into the Diplomatic Service for, despite my deep socialist roots, or rather because of them, I had no illusions about Communism. With a degree in politics I was very familiar with the true nature of totalitarianism and its related temptations for the radical left. But I also knew that my socialism, which grew out of the Welsh Christian community, was founded on democratic principles and had no leanings in that direction.'

His interesting time in Hungary was curtailed when he felt that he wanted to return to his political roots and have the opportunity to stand for parliament. To do this he knew that he had no alternative but to resign from the service. It was a major decision for him, financially and in career terms, for there is little doubt that he would have risen through the ranks to stand alongside his colleagues, many of whom are now ambassadors.

'I resigned in late 1964 to take up a lecturing post at Swansea University and from there I was selected to stand for the marginal seat of Monmouth, then held for the Conservatives by Peter Thorneycroft. We won that seat in 1966, the first time it had been gained by Labour, when there was a tidal wave of victory for the party across the country - a wave which receded to our cost four years later.'

Realising that he had a marginal seat and a baby son to

consider, and finding that there were many dead hours in
parliament when he could either waste time or do something constructive, he decided to read for the Bar. He
studied for three years while maintaining his constituency in Monmouth and he was called to the Bar in 1969.
His being a qualified barrister when he lost his seat by a
narrow margin in 1970, effectively cushioned the blow
and gave him a sense of purpose, as well as affording him
an opportunity which would prove invaluable to him later
in his political life.

'Although I was very keen to return to Westminster, I
did not chase after every by-election which came up but,
when my home seat became available, clearly that was a
great attraction for me; although, as the wags would say,
a 20,000 majority helped! I might have gone for another
seat in Wales but I would not really have wished to go out
of the Principality, no matter how attractive the position
may have been. I practised as a barrister for four years
until 1974 when I won the seat at Swansea East, although
in such "safe" seats, the real battle is to win the selection
in the first place. Here my Swansea background helped
me to get over that hurdle in spite of giving "the wrong
answers to all the questions" - as the leader of the council
told me later.'

To many it must have seemed strange for him to
exchange a comfortable, secure lifestyle as a barrister for
the hectic life of an MP, forced to spend long periods
away from home, under the constant watch of the media
and regularly open to criticism. He countered this sugges-
tion with conviction.

'Granted, the monetary rewards were considerably

less but, as a Christian, I believed then, and still do, that the opportunities for witness and contact with a cross section of society were very much greater. I like to think that I share the prejudices of the constituency I represent and I feel that the job satisfaction is much greater when one is representing one's home area. I know the people around me; I am part of the framework of the community; and feel that I can more easily go the extra mile on their behalf.

'As far as I am concerned, the opportunities as a Christian in politics are very clear. I recall the time when I lost the seat at Monmouth, where I believed I had worked hard and had related well to a cross section of the Christian community. What an encouragement it was for me to receive a large number of letters of appreciation from many of my constituents, including virtually all the local clerics. Earlier I remember receiving warm approval from a local Labour activist and Christian, the local sub-postmaster in Croesyceiliog. Even in the heat of an election campaign, I could truly say that, if it were God's will, I would gladly leave parliament.

'A politician is in the limelight and, therefore, has the potential to witness indirectly. I have access to the media, and the stand which I take as a politician is more widely publicised than that of people in most other professions. That is not to deny, however, that those in journalism, business, teaching or law, for example, can, by their life and witness, live out the Christian message and be ambassadors too.

'With so many people watching your every move, life in politics is like living in a goldfish bowl. Our activities are more widely publicised now than ever before but there is the advantage that it provides us with the opportunity to reach out to a greater number of people. It would be foolish not to realise that this can be for good or ill and, when the politician slips on a banana skin, the world is looking on. It is essential, therefore, that our deeds do not badly reflect the standards we set ourselves, nor the faith we profess.

'If politicians take a clear stand on principle, that also will be seen by more people. I have rarely found that my beliefs have been a problem to me as a member of my party. I like to think that most of the views I hold as a Christian, in terms, for example, of Matthew 25: using one's God-given talents, caring for strangers and those in need; or the general concern for the underdog in society, are reflected largely in the policies of my party. There are certain social issues where "progressive" people in the Labour Party hold views which are contrary to my own but there has been no attempt to drag me into the lobby when it comes to the vote. If ever there were such coercion I would firmly resist, and reject it completely.

'Having been in the Labour Party when it has been in government, and now in opposition, I would say that the temptations and strains for the backbencher are less when in opposition. The major dilemmas would be encountered by a minister in cabinet who feels the tension between loyalty to the government of which he is a part and loyalty to his own beliefs. When one takes on a party label there are certain obligations. People in general do not vote for me because they may think I am a nice person; nor because I am a Christian. They support me because

I represent a particular party. That fact imposes obligations on me not to go off on a frolic or a whim as the
situation takes me.

'If my party tried to impose a social agenda which was
contrary to my Christian commitment, that would indeed
be a dilemma, but most of the issues in relation to marriage, the family etc. are largely left to individual conscience. These are the so-called "Friday issues" which
come up on that day of the week. Whether it be abortion,
attitudes to sexuality or the like, they are viewed as
matters of conscience which the individual must decide
according to his or her own personal beliefs, whatever the
official party line. As far as I am concerned, I have never
found myself in a situation of one hundred per cent
conflict, but if that ever did occur, it would be a matter of
balancing my obligations to the party with my commitment to the Christian principles which I adhere to and, of
course, selecting with care the issue or issues on which I
should take a stand.

'Generally speaking, political decisions do not come
as absolutes: but the mere fact that this is the case is also
partly a dilemma for me. At times I feel that the Christian
community may assume that we march into parliament
with the banner of Christ and every decision thereafter is
measured as *for* or *against* Christian ideals. My principles are certainly a guide but most of the decisions I have
to take are not in the realm of absolutes but will be
relative, more so or less so.

'For example, as far as Sunday trading is concerned,
I happen to be patron of "Keep Sunday Special" and I
have my own views on Sunday as a day of rest and

recreation. I believe that this is not only good for me but makes good sense for everyone else. Many of the laws related to the individual in the Old Testament have been scorned but, considered objectively, can be seen to be right precepts in human terms and also in the context of current hygiene practices. Advice on personal hygiene in the Old Testament is a good example of this.

'But when we come to translating that to a non-Christian society it is a question, not of absolutes nor indeed of imposing our view, but of recognising that Christian values are right. They have to be "sold" to the community at large as being worthy of their acceptance. The whole idea of raising the standards of the nation is one way of underpinning the values that we believe are right for society.

'I believe that much of the social wreckage we see around us is a direct result of the abandonment of Christian standards, whether it be of family values; or in relation to violence on television; or pornography. Just as what we ingest nutritionally has an effect on our bodies, so I am sure that what we take in through the mind via literature and television has an effect on our attitude to other people. I feel that it is my duty to try to make a Christian input into debates in those areas. As much as I deprecate the loosening of family ties and consequences such as the explosion of one-parent families, I shall still campaign vigorously against social conditions which weigh heavily on such persons in need.

'In a democracy, one cannot impose one's views on these matters, but one can try to win over society to accept their worth for the greater good. Happily, I think there is some evidence that attitudes are changing as people see the social cost of the rejection of these values. The consequences of family break-up is but one example. I firmly believe that only by looking at these issues, as it were through Christian spectacles, can we see them more clearly defined and be ready to respond but in a rounded way.

'One of my friends, Michael Schluter, who is the director of the Jubilee Centre at Cambridge, has recently co-authored a book about relationships.[1] Human relationships are of immense importance to a healthy society and are the building blocks upon which everything depends. Anything that can be done by way of government policy to strengthen these relationships will be of benefit to the community at large.

'By contrast, any decisions taken in parliament, which are seen to mar or fragment those relationships will have adverse social consequences. I feel, therefore, that it is incumbent on us to try to look at policy across the board through Christian spectacles and to struggle to get as much of that accepted, using arguments which may not necessarily be Christian, as one must appeal beyond Christian circles.'

These principles have gained him considerable respect, not only in his constituency, where he now has an unassailable majority of over twenty-three thousand, but also during his life in parliament. He has held a number of posts including: Parliamentary Private Secretary to the Minister of Defence (1969-70) and to the Attorney General (1974-79); Chairman of the Select Committee on Welsh Affairs; Opposition Front Bench Spokesman on Foreign and Commonwealth Affairs for ten years.

Building on his experience as a diplomat he has had the opportunity to be an officer of the British/French, British/German, British/Norwegian and British/Zimbabwe Parliamentary Groups. In 1986 he was honoured with the Commander's Cross of the Order of Merit of the Federal Republic of Germany for contribution to British/German relationships. He has been the senior Labour Member of both the Commonwealth Parliamentary Association and of the Inter-Parliamentary Union and has been for the ten years since its foundation, Senior Vice President of AWEPA which began as a campaigning anti-apartheid organisation and is now a development pressure group for Africa among the parliamentarians of Europe.

During his time in the House he has been an active supporter of the National Prayer Breakfast, which he chaired in 1989 and of the Parliamentary Christian Fellowship of which he has been chairman since 1990. He spoke of the value he puts on this fellowship within Westminster.

'The House of Commons Christian Fellowship is an important place of retreat, a time to step aside from the pressures around us. Yes, we do have our political differences and I confess that I find it difficult to understand how my Conservative colleagues hold certain views and they, no doubt, have similar difficulties with my political standpoint! But we have a forum to debate them in the House and feel that we can lay these issues aside for a time to share friendship and fellowship as well as searching for that common ground on which there is much we can build.

'It is also a time to share experiences and to minister to those, in and out of the faith, because people experiencing personal tragedy are at their most needy and are more receptive to help and Christian support. In my judgment that is an important part of the Christian commitment. As we recognise the oneness of people because all are created by God in His image, and as we accept that God is concerned for all people, we also realise that Christians are ambassadors for Christ. Their mission is to feed His sheep in recognition of their own debt to Him. As God reminded the Israelites: *Remember that you were bondsmen in Egypt, therefore I command you to do this thing.* So also this should be the spur to our involvement with other people.'

Life in parliament is a potential destroyer of family life but some of the pressures on home life, which an MP inevitably encounters, have been alleviated to a certain extent by Donald's ability to maintain a home in London and in Wales. But it has led to divided loyalties as far as church work is concerned. We discussed how he has coped with this.

'I have such an artificial lifestyle, living between Swansea and London. In London, we worship at a local Anglican church, under the ministry of Andrew Watson, if anything because it is the most lively church near us. When we are in Swansea we worship in the United Reformed Church, where Kevin Watson is the minister but I also do some preaching in churches of different denominations so I could be said to be fairly ecumenical in my outlook!'

Whatever he has turned his hand to, be it diplomat,

barrister or parliamentarian, Donald Anderson has always been dedicated and committed to carry out the task
to the best of his ability. He left me in no doubt that he will
continue to use these gifts as long as there is a job to be
done and he has the health and strength to carry on.

1. *The R Factor*. Michael Schluter and David Lee, (Hodder and Stoughton, 1993)

8

BETTY MAWHINNEY
Parliamentary Wives Group

Partners in Prayer

When interviewing Members of Parliament a number of
them talked about the challenge of finding time to be with
their families, given the hectic schedule at Westminster
and in their constituencies. They spoke of the pressures,
not only on themselves but also on their wives, who may
be left at home to bring up children or look after elderly
relatives, and who can experience a loneliness unique to
their situation. While MPs are the ones elected to take a
seat in the House, their partners find themselves playing
a supporting role with which it is not always easy to come
to terms. In this connection, a number of MPs referred to
the ministry in the House of Commons of the Parliamentary Wives Group. I decided to learn more about them.

One who is particularly involved in this group is Betty
Mawhinney, wife of Dr Brian Mawhinney, Conservative
MP for Peterborough. He was Minister of State for Health
before becoming a Cabinet Member as Transport Secretary. Betty very kindly invited me to their home to tell me
about her life and to describe the role that she has played
in recent years, in support of her husband, and among the
wives of his fellow MPs.

She was born in Detroit, Michigan, USA, an only

child. Although her parents did not attend church regularly they sent her to the local Presbyterian Sunday School. When she later attended the University of Michigan, to study for a nursing degree, she came into contact with the Inter-Varsity Christian Fellowship, who invited her to attend various meetings which they had organised.

'I met there a group of young people who had a joy and a sense of purpose in life which I knew nothing about. I was greatly attracted by the fellowship and friendship which they offered me. Some time later I was asked to join a Nurses Christian Fellowship camp and was touched by the preaching of the late Paul Little, a worker with the Inter-Varsity Fellowship and author of a number of books on evangelism. He had a wonderful gift of communicating the gospel and it was explained to me in a way that I was able to understand for the first time. Before I left that camp, I committed myself to Christ and my life became very different thereafter.

'I completed the four year course at university and, in my final year, met Brian Mawhinney, a student from Northern Ireland, who had been doing a bachelor's degree at Queen's University, Belfast. As part of an exchange programme with Michigan, he won a scholarship to study for a year in the States and he too attended the Christian Union. When he had completed his year with us, he returned to Belfast to continue his studies. We kept in touch and, the following Christmas, we were engaged to be married.'

They were married in Michigan the following year and set up home in London, a city that Betty had not visited before, where Brian was working on his PhD in

Radiation Biology. When he completed his studies, he was offered a post as assistant professor at the University of Iowa. Once again, this time with a baby son, Betty was back across the Atlantic in her home country. They lived there for three years, after which they returned to Britain when Brian was invited to lecture at London University. Politics was the last thing on their minds at that time but a chain of events would soon take place which would change their lives dramatically and show them a path which they believed God meant them to follow.

'When we returned to England, we became involved in Cholmeley Evangelical Church in North London, where Brian was an elder. It was at that time that he wished to broaden his interests. He joined the local Conservative Association. Though previous to this Brian had shown little interest in becoming involved in politics, shortly afterwards he was asked by a close friend, who was a candidate for a seat in the North of England, to support him with canvassing in Northumberland, when the General Election was called in February 1974. He agreed to do so.

'He was out and about in the area speaking to people in the local market when he was engaged in a long conversation with a woman who turned out to be the Conservative agent for the North East of England. She became very insistent that he should apply to be a candidate, somehow believing that he had what it took!

'Brian was quite taken aback by this and declined to take the invitation further at that time. "Well, at least send me your curriculum vitae," she insisted. He said he would do so when he returned home to London.'

They heard nothing more and, in July, Betty and Brian went off to the States to visit her folks in Michigan, putting the incident to the back of their minds. When they came back home there was a pile of letters behind the door from several constituencies saying 'Thank you for applying to be our parliamentary candidate, but we are sorry that, on this occasion, you have not been selected.'

The same evening that they returned to find the unexpected correspondence, Brian received a phone call from the chairman of the Conservative Association in Stockton-on-Tees. Betty recalled the conversation:

' "Dr Mawhinney, I have received your application to be a candidate in our constituency...," the man said, before Brian interrupted with, "Well, that's interesting because I was not aware that I had applied." "Oh, yes," continued the caller, "we have your application, together with all your details. Would you be willing to come up for an interview?"

'It is an understatement to say that we were stunned! Brian had made it clear to the lady he chanced to meet at the market in Blyth that he was not pushing to become an MP. On receipt of his CV she had clearly felt that he was giving the go-ahead for her to send his details to a number of Conservative associations.'

Betty went on to describe further their reaction to this turn of events.

'I had no real political interests at all at that time and neither of us had a background which would have fostered any enthusiasm for the subject. We were complete novices and here we were being pursued by a constituency to stand for selection. Was this pure coincidence or was God trying to tell us something? I knew that Brian was keen to widen his horizons, take up a new challenge, so I went along with it somewhat half-heartedly, quite happy for him to "dabble" if he wished to do so. But, what I thought would be a passing phase, turned out to be something which would change our lives.

'After that phone call we began to take it more seriously, wondering if this was a direction that God indeed wanted us to take. We had three young children at this stage and it certainly would be a decision which would affect the whole family.'

Brian and Betty discussed it for some time, prayed about it and became convinced that it was a door which was opening for them. At least they should give it a push and find out what happened. If this was not the direction which God wanted them to take, they prayed that the door would close and that would be the end of it.

'Brian went up to Stockton-on-Tees for the interview; he was short-listed and invited to go forward for selection. We were surprised and pleased when he was chosen but there already had been an election that year so thought that it would be some time before he would have to make any moves. A week after he was selected, a second General Election was called!'

Thrown in at the political deep end, Brian duly fought the campaign to the best of his ability. He was not really surprised when he was soundly defeated by William Rodgers, the Labour Cabinet Minister, later one of the Liberal Democrat 'Gang of Four'. Despite his lack of success, the local association were full of praise for his efforts and encouraged him to press on and apply to be put on the party's official candidates list.

'It had been an interesting experience for us and Brian had enjoyed it. Perhaps this was the way God wanted us to follow. We talked about it further and decided that, since Brian had a commitment to the university, and we had to take account of our family responsibilities, he should only consider being a candidate for a safe or marginal seat within travelling distance of our home in London.'

Within a short time, Brian began to receive details of vacancies and he applied to half a dozen, including Peterborough, which he was invited to join as a candidate from a list of 93 hopefuls.

'Again, we were amazed, given Brian's limited political experience locally and nationally, and our lack of involvement in wider Conservative circles. On top of that I was American, he was from Northern Ireland and we had never been to Peterborough before the invitation to attend for interview. By all accounts, we had little going for us. Even the local paper in Peterborough had a headline and comment to that effect.'

Against all the odds, it seemed to them, Brian won the seat by a clear majority at the General Election in 1979 and he has held it ever since. If the run up to the election caused dramatic changes in the life of the Mawhinneys, it was nothing compared to the challenges they would face after winning. Betty had married a talented lecturer and researcher and now she was to be the wife of an MP, with all the disruption to family life which that entailed. As one person put it, she would be 'joining the ranks of the Westminster Widows', a cynical reference to the loneliness which the wives of many MPs experience, particularly in the early years.

We discussed how she reacted to her new role and the effect that it had on family life. She spoke also of new opportunities afforded to her and the support she has found through her Christian faith and in fellowship with other wives in similar circumstances.

'I was far from being on the sideline during all this as I had to go through an interview, no doubt to assess my "suitability" as a candidate's wife. It was quite nerve-racking for me but I came through, not only unscathed, but encouraged. There was only one question: "In what way are you able to support your husband in the constituency?" I explained that I would support my husband by going to Peterborough as often as I could but made the point that I felt that the best support I could offer him was to stay in London and care for our three children to maintain a stable home life. I was unsure what their reaction would be to that but, after I had had my say, I was rather surprised when I received a standing ovation!

'All things considered and, despite the upheaval in our family life, I could not deny that the chain of events had been remarkable and it seemed that this was where God wanted us to be at that time in our lives. This helped me considerably as it was certainly not what I would have chosen to do. The family have not only survived, but have thrived, and our children are now well adjusted, sensible adults of whom we are proud. They are all committed Christians and that has been a great joy for us. Our elder son, David, is working in China at the moment, teaching English at a university: the second, Stephen, who did a degree in Politics and Economics at Oxford, is a journalist with ITN; and our daughter, Alison, has also just finished a degree in Politics and Economics at Bristol.

'When we moved house, we continued to travel regularly to our former place of worship but it was half an hour's drive towards the city and we felt that we should join the lively local Anglican church which is within walking distance of our home and had many activities for our children. It was a difficult move for us to make as we had so many good friends at Cholmeley. We are regular attenders at services but, with my other Christian work in the House, I am not involved in as many of the church activities as I was able to be before. There is a local interdenominational Bible study group in our home area which I like to support. In addition, there are political commitments which I have, including being president of the Conservative Women's Association in Peterborough, which takes me there about three times a month.

'One of the first things I had to get used to was Brian's frequent absences from home during the week and at weekends. I often had to cope alone with school events and many of the other things that couples may do together with their children. We did debate at that time whether we should move to Peterborough but felt that, since he had to be in London most of the week, that was where we should stay. As least he was able to come home more often than those MPs whose constituencies are far from Westminster.

'I feel very much for many of Brian's colleagues and their spouses. To some extent this has been a spur for me to become involved in supporting them. Many have a different story from mine, and for some it has been very much more difficult, particularly if they have not had a similar sense of calling to the job as husband and wife, as we have been privileged to have.

'The Parliamentary Wives Group was formed in 1977, a couple of years before we appeared on the scene. Sylvia Mary Alison, wife of Michael Alison MP, was the one to whom God gave a vision for the ministry. She longed for an all-party group of parliamentary wives to meet to study the Bible and to pray, as she had seen amongst American Congress wives. At a church Bible study one evening she discussed it with another wife; they invited some others they thought might be interested and six of them met. They prayed and talked together all one summer.

'The immediate problem was deciding where they could meet as there were no spare rooms within the House itself. With some trepidation, they approached George Thomas, the Speaker at that time, as he had made it known he would love to see the Speaker's House used in some way for Christian work and fellowship. They asked if he would allow them to use a room, having in mind also that this would be "neutral" ground, as it had no party political connections. He very graciously agreed, and a dozen or so members' wives started to meet every Tuesday lunchtime. The primary aim was to support each other, to build each other up in the Body of Christ, by praying and studying the Bible together.

'We still meet informally each week with growing numbers, usually with a speaker who gives a Bible based talk, followed by questions and discussion. Another group

also meets in the evening, as some wives have outside
work or, for other reasons, cannot attend at midday. A
number of peers' wives have joined us, and there is also
a group of women whose husbands have left the House,
having retired or died recently. From a small gathering
with a big vision, it has developed into a network of
people with a wider vision than even the founders might
have anticipated.

'Aware that many MPs' wives do not live within easy
reach of Westminster and that a number have family or
career commitments, which may prevent them from joining us, we feel that we ought to consider branching out to
form regional groups. We have been to Wales and there
are burgeoning groups in the North West of England and
in other parts of the country. A few of us went up to
Scotland when Billy Graham was there and we were able
to organise a lunch with Ruth Graham to which we
invited all the Scottish parliamentary wives. A good
number came and we have kept in touch with them since.

'The aim of the fellowship is not just to support those
who are committed Christians, but to be a help to all who
wish to come along, whatever their persuasion, and to
provide a forum for discussion of many aspects of our
lives. We do not hide our Christian principles but neither
do we put pressure on anyone to make a commitment, nor
give the impression that only Christians are welcome to
join. However, some who have come along and been
helped have become Christians as a result.

'From time to time we organise events for wider
outreach, perhaps a lunch or a coffee morning, and out of
that a number have come to know the Lord. We have a

supper party for MPs in Speaker's House, which we arrange about three times a year. The Speakers have been very supportive of what we are doing and some have kept us up to date with matters for prayer, such as the illness of a member or one of the wives, or some other family problem.

'When the current Speaker, Betty Boothroyd, was appointed I wrote to her to explain the work we were doing. She has very kindly continued to support us by letting us use her House and she occasionally looks in when we are meeting. Sometimes we get requests to make visits to support members who are experiencing difficulties in their lives. I recall one recently when it seemed that there was a serious possibility of a breakdown in their marriage. We offered them our counsel and prayers and like to think that we have been able to help them to stay together.

'There are other examples, which confidentiality will not allow me to discuss, but you read about some of them in the newspapers. We always try to help out whatever the situation, or the accusation, if we can do so without seeming to intrude or interfere. Some have approached us personally and asked for prayer. We may write a letter, perhaps make a phone call, depending on the request, or the need which has been brought to our attention. It is so easy to forget that MPs and their wives are no less vulnerable than others, simply because of their special position in society. They have the same pressures, and more, because of that position; have the same temptations, times of despair and loneliness which others experience. Because of their public position, however, they may not always know to whom to turn for help and advice and there is always the fear that the media will pick up a grain of truth and make something greater out of it.

'Confidentiality is of utmost importance if people are to feel free to come to us to ask for help and prayer. We constantly remind each other of this when we meet. And so a real pastoral role is developing, not just within our group but within the Houses of Parliament in general.

'It has been a great source of encouragement for us to know that we are widely respected. I would be naive if I did not realise that some may see us as a quaint little women's clique: the same people who may frown upon the House of Commons Christian Fellowship; but we are encouraged, nevertheless, by the general acceptance which is growing year by year. There is such a difference in the overall response to the group, from the beginnings in 1977, to what it is today. It has become a part of life in the House of Commons in a way which has surprised many. We stress that, while we are apolitical, we are not afraid to make our voice heard if issues concern us; but not to the extent of lobbying or banner waving! We are more likely to tell our husbands about our concerns and leave it to them to raise it in the House, if appropriate.

'However, that is far from being our primary role and we steer clear of controversial, party political issues. Our main purpose is to build each other up spiritually through pastoral work, Bible study and prayer. We have organised, sometimes with a bit of difficulty, seminars where we invite people who have some expertise in an area of legislation that is going through the House and which has some particular Christian connotation. We invite members of our fellowship, and others who are interested, to come along.

'The difficulty in organising the meeting springs from our awareness that, when we do so, we may unintentionally be bordering on the contentious, and our venue in the Speaker's House would preclude this form of discussion. It has always been difficult to find a place to have these occasional meetings, which are not really meant to be contentious, but are aimed at educating us on the facts behind the issues. I would wish to stress again that these are exceptional occasions, as we do not consider that the majority of issues necessarily have a clear, unequivocal Christian line, with which all Christian politicians could agree. But we do pray that, at all times, whatever the area for discussion in the House, God's will shall be done.'

For those who have little or no contact with the House of Commons, other than through the media, it may come as a great surprise to learn that Westminster, a seemingly distant, frequently controversial place, where the nation's decision-makers meet, is also a place of prayer and fellowship. Members of Parliament have spoken to me of the help they find in the House of Commons Christian Fellowship. The interesting work of the Parliamentary Wives group is yet another tier of support.

God has blessed the work they are doing and it has grown. Betty and her friends are not content to leave things as they are but have a vision that it should continue to grow, touch an even greater number of people, and not only in London. The formation of groups for those partners who are not able to meet with them in Speaker's House is one encouraging example. With Europe in-

creasingly taking centre stage, the thought of expanding
in that direction has also crossed their minds.

Much of what they do cannot be recorded here and
some of it only a handful of people are aware of, but their
work, at the heart of the nation, is certainly worthy of our
prayers.

9
JOHN G. MUIR

A House Divided.......?

I learned that a well-known BBC journalist once commented, 'Interviewing politicians can be like nailing custard to the wall,' and I began to wonder what I had embarked upon when I agreed to write this book. I have to confess also that, prior to setting out for Westminster to meet the Members of Parliament who kindly agreed to contribute, I had mixed views on politics generally and on the intentions of politicians in particular. Opinion polls on the subject would indicate that I was not alone in my cynicism, a large number of the populace placing politicians low down in their estimation of trustworthiness.

Several interviews later I now admit to being impressed with the valuable work being done by many on our behalf at Westminster and at the same time more conscious of the frustrations which members experience when faced with dilemmas in society today. This is particularly so among opposition MPs who feel unable to effect change in the country under a Government so long in power and which even its supporters acknowledge has pushed through some controversial legislation on the strength of its majority in Parliament.

A selection of Christian politicians from left, right and centre took time to explain to me the challenges which they face from day to day. Their shared beliefs and common ground for friendships and fellowship encouraged me greatly. As you have read their accounts you will have reached your own conclusions. I could not help but note, however, that they live under the constraint of divided loyalties, a problem highlighted as they expressed why they believe that their political party viewpoint showed the way towards a solution to the problems facing the United Kingdom.

Although it could be argued that there has been concern about the direction our country has been taking for some time, it seems to me that this has been particularly so since the election in 1992. As I spoke to MPs I became convinced that, to a great extent, parliament has suffered from the same problems which have beset the country at large. I refer to the sense of hopelessness and depression. Political life at Westminster has been bogged down with a number of negatives.

There has been a mixed reaction to European policy, we have experienced recession in the economy as a whole and there is national dismay at the growth in unemployment. Add to that the sense of despair with the political situation in Northern Ireland and there is no need to go out into the highways and byways or read the result of opinion polls to sense that people feel increasingly alienated from the decision makers, currently the Conservatives, a party which seems intent also in tearing itself apart in public.

In case I am accused of being 'against the Government' as I write, I get the impression that the proverbial man or woman in the street is yet to be convinced that another party in power would not be similarly fraught with factions.

There is certainly a feeling across the country that the nation is leaderless and without any clear sense of direction. In addition there has been a decline in respect for many of our established institutions: such as the monarchy, with the widely reported break up of royal marriages; the established Church with its drastic decrease in membership and influence; and the legal system with media coverage of a number of miscarriages of justice and apparently inappropriate sentencing of offenders.

There is considerable despair about the way many of our young people live and about the failure of the education and welfare services to address the concerns. Where once there were clear standards of character and behaviour that were observed at all levels of society, there seems to be decline. Not unnaturally, this has led to a feeling of depression, highlighted in recent times by the public self examination of our society following the conviction of two primary age children for the murder of a toddler. 'Can this be true?' is the cry which goes up across the land as people pinch themselves in the hope that it is all a bad dream.

When things go wrong we search for someone to blame. It may be the turn of schools and teachers to be given the stick or perhaps the inefficiency of the police is suggested as a cause. So the politicians rush to introduce legislation which will placate the electorate. In its haste the Government often alienates the very professionals whose cooperation and trust are needed to effect meaningful change.

Again the failure of the Church on the one hand to take a firm stand on issues of morality has been criticised while on the other hand the clergy has been blamed for dabbling too frequently in politics, particularly when politicians don't care for their message. The tendency among some MPs to try to neatly separate the secular from the spiritual seems to the sceptical to be as much an attempt to stifle criticism of 'unpopular' political action as it is to put the Church in its place. The reference to 'Render unto Caesar ...' is more of an excuse - a manipulation of the words of Christ - than a reason, in such circumstances.

In this regard I find myself agreeing with Montefiore when he said:

> 'The effect of government policies on people is the proper concern of churchmen, especially when people, by their poverty and powerlessness, are unable to speak for themselves.'[1]

There has been no shortage of publications over the past ten years in which parliamentarians on both sides of the House have expressed their views on Christian principles as reflected by their particular political beliefs. The tendency for protagonists to appear to manipulate scripture (taking a text out of context and using it as a pretext!) to explain or justify their political stance has only served to confuse Christians and non-Christians alike and effectively underline the divisions rather than highlight the common ground. The now famous 'Sermon on the Mound', when Margaret Thatcher spoke to the General Assembly of the Church of Scotland, is but one celebrated example which sparked off a debate beyond the pews of the Kirk.

From time to time we point to the media as the ones who should bear some of the blame for parading the failures in society rather than the successes. There are cries for good news to be given prominence rather than bad when we switch on our televisions or pick up the newspaper.

Whatever we identify as being the root cause of, or even the main contributor to, the current depressing state of the nation, no one can deny that the total impact is a more acute breakdown of our social fabric than has been noted at any time since the last world war. Where even ten years ago there were stable factors in society upon which people could depend, there is now a lack of stability and no clear leadership emerging to steady the boat. I was greatly encouraged to find so many fine Christian people in the House of Commons taking a stand on issues of morality and personal belief but, at the end of my time with them, I remained concerned with the lack of direction which seemed to prevail in Westminster as a whole.

The 'shared beliefs' among Christians in the House which became evident to me after meeting MPs were at times overshadowed by their obvious 'divided loyalties'. It seemed to me that parliament, rather than being at the helm to chart the way ahead for the nation with ideas and policies as much as legislation, may be in danger of losing its way in the fog of political rhetoric. The voters are justified in being sceptical and critical of a system which fails to deliver what they voted for. Party Manifestos published for election purposes lose their impact as 'climbdowns' and 'U-turns' undermine their validity.

Just as worrying is the fact that the electorate do not appear to trust parliament to lead us out of the fog. The result is that, for MPs, including those who profess to be Christian, the task has been one of considerable pain. For many MPs it has often been a struggle, arguing over issues which many of them do not feel are right or even fully understand. Some have also been challenged to compromise their own positions for the sake of party unity. Clearly, what is taking place is more a reflection of the decline of government than in any period for decades. Parliamentarians seem to have lost their way.

None of the MPs I spoke to attempted to give one definitive 'Christian' answer to the malaise and neither did I expect them to do so. Some did point to the need for the nation to return to the faith of our forefathers, a faith which is outgoing, underpinned by a respect for the individual and one which stresses spiritual as well as moral values. All of them spoke of the centrality of their own faith to their experience.

Off the record, some alluded to the fact that many of their colleagues confess not to know where they are going nor are they sure how to proceed in the immediate future. In a nutshell, the social and economic problems besetting our country seem to be more numerous than the solutions available to manage them. There is an overwhelming sense that hands are being thrown up in desperation.

Uppermost in everyone's mind at present is the imbalance in the economy; the fact that Britain has got itself into such serious debt that it cannot be resolved by simply reviewing taxation policy alone. Then there is the issue of crime and crime prevention when people believe, rightly or wrongly, that law and order has broken down in the streets of our towns and cities. Men and women speak of living in fear in society, despite large increases in expenditure for policing. It is worrying that voters do not believe that politicians can offer any credible solution to the problems besetting us. Sadly, it is the perception of a large section of the electorate that the Government seems to be reinforcing this viewpoint by offering yesterday's ideas for the problems of today.

In the light of this situation in the United Kingdom, it would be helpful, I believe, if Christian MPs in all parties took a stand when all around them are in despair. Contact with some of them encouraged me that it is possible. Despite the barracking and bantering that goes on among them, the truth is that politicians of all shades of opinion are aware that things are going badly adrift. They too are afraid of the consequences.

Having weighed up the comments by the members I was privileged to meet, and notwithstanding the political pressures exerted upon them, inside and outside the House, I am persuaded that now is the time for MPs who hold to Christian values, whatever their denominational commitment, to dispense with party divides and find a common political platform. The crisis in the nation is unlikely to be resolved by replacing one economic policy with another or substituting the Government's ideas for social change for any of those put forward by opposition parties. It is rather a crisis of leadership with the absence of clear thinking and ideas that are workable. Things are so severe that people thrash around wondering what to do next and are themselves hopelessly depressed.

The Conservatives have been in power since 1979 and I believe that Christians in that party have a unique responsibility to constructively criticize their government. The fact is that, no matter how good things were in the 1980s, a lot of people feel that they are very bad in the 1990s. As they see it, hard times, with recession and a huge number of unemployed, have occurred under the same government, despite their having the power to change it all.

It means that Christian MPs need to be more firm and effective critics of their own policy despite the application of the whip on the floor of the House. If this results in more rebels rising to their feet, so be it. Whatever one's personal views on the Maastricht debate, it is, nevertheless, encouraging to see MPs fighting on matters of belief and conscience, not accepting something because it reflects party dogma. Were there to be further rebellion on other key issues it may ignite a sense of enthusiasm in the nation that parliamentarians actually care more about what offends their neighbours than about what bugs their colleagues in the party.

I recognise that it is difficult for Christian MPs because many of them are ambitious, indeed spiritually ambitious, to gain promotion to be able to influence their party. By all accounts that is laudable but the party machine says that the way to climb the greasy pole is to keep your mouth shut and toe the party line. Were the nation in a position of strength, were the institutions at a point of stability and the poor in the country adequately catered for, there may well be a case for silently observing the difficulties. But this is not the situation at present.

I believe that our nation has passed the point of potential collapse and, if this is the case, Christian MPs are courting a dilemma which many are at a loss to know how to get out of. As I recorded their views I was convinced that they are certainly serving to the best of their ability, fighting hard in their corner but I could not but sense the despair among many of them that they seem to be achieving less than they hoped for.

The MPs I spoke to who are currently in opposition to the present government, conveyed their own particular frustrations, as they count their losses, not only after elections but on the floor of the House. It must affect the motivation of Labour MPs in particular as hopes of being in government have been dashed time and time again. They cannot grab the agenda because they do not seem to have ideas which capture the imagination of sufficient of the electorate to allow them to win. So they try to trip up the Government but do not succeed in effecting real changes in policy. They plod on, hoping that their popularity will turn into a majority at the polls - next time round.

MPs in the other minority parties are no less frustrated as they limp hopefully from one by-election to the next striving to find common ground which allows them to support the Government one day or effectively undermine the ruling party another day.

It is hard to write in this way without being accused of being party political in one's comments but it is my view that, because of the way which British politics has evolved in the course of the last decade, particularly during the

Thatcher years, the need for consensus politics is more urgent than ever before. The old party divides have proved to be insensitive and destructive.

Paddy Ashdown, Liberal Democrat leader, is reported to have said, 'Westminster is dead from the neck up. People are ahead of politicians. Politicians are behind, yet their job is to lead.' It would be easy to dismiss this as simply another example of political rhetoric: but it does seem that people in the country are not convinced that parties have more credible solutions than individuals have. It will not be parties which show the way forward in the years ahead but leaders who are willing to stand up for what they believe and carry their policies through for the benefit of the nation as a whole.

Neither can we ignore the place of Europe in the equation of British politics. If, as some hope and others fear, the development of a European super state is on the cards, with the attendant pressure to integrate and merge institutions and policies, all these factors add up to mean that what takes place in Westminster will become less and less relevant. Instead, what happens in Brussels and Strasbourg will be what affects us most. It is, therefore, very important for politicians on all sides to realise that, in the future, it is possible that their power base in parliament will diminish. An alliance on core common interests may turn out to be more significant than fighting party battles!

When our country faced an external enemy during the Second World War, a coalition government was formed. As we now face an internal enemy, in the form of severe economic, moral and spiritual decline in the state of our nation, this must surely be the point in time to pool our best ideas, bring together effective leaders from all sides of politics and form a coalition for the benefit of the people. The time for truth and leadership is more vital than is standing firm on the grounds of parliamentary procedure or political expediency.

It is hard to determine how this can possibly come about. Perhaps a consideration of existing opportunities may point a way forward. It is not only in the forum of the House of Commons Christian Fellowship that political differences are laid aside. Issues of conscience and belief are generally debated openly with the removal of the whip when it comes to a vote. Indeed, as evidenced by MPs I interviewed, when the party in power has attempted to push through legislation which does not reflect the consensus view of its members, applying the whip has frequently failed to be effective. At a time of crisis in our country why should not consensus across party lines be sought when debates concentrate on issues which may be socially and economically divisive or when legislation may be seen to be undermining the moral fabric of the nation?

Precedents have already been set in existing cross-party committees and delegations which debate issues of general interest or when MPs travel together on fact-finding missions. These and similar forums were valued by all the MPs I spoke to. Of particular interest to me was the opportunity afforded to interested MPs by the recently formed Movement For Christian Democracy.

There are other occasions when political barriers between MPs lose their significance. When the untimely

death of the Rt. Hon. John Smith, Leader of the Labour
Party, was announced to a hushed House of Commons
one could not but be impressed with the conduct of MPs
on both sides of the House. Viewers and listeners accus-
tomed to noisy scenes, reflecting the normal adversarial
nature of British politics, witnessed instead a totally
civilised gathering of men and women united in their
grief at the passing of a colleague and friend. Even the
media seemed taken aback with the contrast.

Perhaps for the first time for many it came across how
differences could be laid aside in the search for common
purpose. Interview after interview revealed how 'oppo-
nents' did not mean 'enemies' and how friendships and
common goals have developed over the years between
apparent foes. The caring side of those who represent us,
of which I was aware during my time with the contributors to this book, became evident to the world at large. I
believe that this picture of unity among MPs may well
have done more to foster respect for our politicians than
any other event in recent times. Accepting that it would be
unrealistic under our present system for such conduct to
be the 'norm' within debate at Westminster, perhaps if
this respect were to be maintained by further acts of
common purpose for the benefit of the country as a whole,
politics may yet be rescued from the present malaise.

Yet the onus for the identification of a 'rescue pack-
age' for our country must surely lie, not only with MPs
generally or Christian MPs in particular, but also with
every individual in society. If we care for our country we
must also be bold to write to our MPs, to express our
views convincingly and, as far as possible, devoid of any

political or religious narrowness which may cause our plea to be rejected without reference. 'The silent majority' has always existed. It was there in Hitler's and Mussolini's day; behind The Iron Curtain and beyond; until, more often than not, it became the 'silenced majority'.

Often we speak impersonally of 'society', 'parliament' or 'the Government' as we urge 'them' to do something to improve our lot. We speak of 'the Church' yet we know that it not just a building but is made up of individuals, be it clergy or laity. National political action may be necessary but so also is the need for Christians to live and love as Christ portrayed in the Gospels. As the Bible insists, we must also pray with and for those in authority over us. For us, that can encompass the Government and Members of Parliament, whether or not they share our political or spiritual aspirations. It is important that we have politicians with intelligence and wisdom to allow them to operate effectively. At the same time we must pray that those whose values and beliefs reflect Christian principles will be willing to stand for Parliament to swell the numbers of those already there. By doing so, this is but one important way we can become partners in politics.

The sense of despair being experienced in our land as I write, while disturbing, may yet prove to be the catalyst for the salvation of our nation, politically and spiritually. Apathy and failure to be aware of the need for healing in our country would be far worse. As Christ said, 'Only the sick have need of a physician.'

1. *Christianity and Politics*, Hugh Montefiore (The MacMillan Press 1990)

O Lord, all the world belongs to you,
And you are always making all things new.
What is wrong you forgive,
And the new life you give
Is what is turning the world upside down.

The world lives divided and apart,
You draw us together, and we start
In our friendship to see
That in harmony we
Can be turning the world upside down.

P. Appleford